The
STANFORD

Health & Exercise

HANDBOOK

The STANFORD
Health & Exercise
HANDBOOK

Developed by the
Stanford Alumni Association
in conjunction with the
Stanford Center for Research in
Disease Prevention

Foreword by
John W. Farquhar, M.D.

Editorial Director
Tony Evans, Ph.D.

Leisure Press
Champaign, Illinois

Note

In several chapters where more than one author is involved authorship is shared equally by the contributors.

Library of Congress Catalog Card Number 87-62863

ISBN: 0-88011-366-9

© 1987 by the Stanford Alumni Association

Co-published in 1989 by Leisure Press,
A Division of Human Kinetics Publishers

Cover Design: Jack Davis
Printed By: Malloy

Printed in the United States of America

10 9 8 7 6 5 4 3 2 1

Co-published with the Stanford Alumni Association by
Leisure Press
A Division of Human Kinetics Publishers, Inc.
Box 5076, Champaign, IL 61825-5076
1-800-342-5457
1-800-334-3665 (in Illinois)

Contents

Foreword

by John W. Farquhar, M.D.

*I*n a time of high-tech inventions and in a region that is world-famous for their development – the Stanford University and Silicon Valley area of California – we have lost sight of the fact that the greatest high-tech invention of all time is the human body. Even though it has been 300 years since Dr. William Harvey described the circulation of the blood, a simple bit of basic science to us today, countless mysteries of the human body remain to be discovered. We can put a man on the moon and occasionally go to the Rose Bowl, but we are only beginning to describe and quantify the miracle of the human machine.

In my 30 years as a physician, I am increasingly amazed at the abuse inflicted indifferently, and sometimes deliberately, on the body. We tend to ignore our responsibility for its maintenance and the consequences of our actions. We arrogantly assume that malfunction will strike the other fellow, never ourselves.

Today we know that habits and lifestyle influence our health, that what we are born with is not what we will die with. Along the way from birth to death our arteries get clogged, our lungs polluted, our organs diseased, our muscles atrophied. Health is a natural resource, and like other natural resources, we should make every effort to preserve it. Most of us are born into this world as perfect machines; but long before we leave this world our high-tech appearance and performance changes for the worse. We are beset with all the problems that flesh is heir to.

Is this march toward illness and decrepitude inevitable, or can we do something to prevent our own obsolescence? What threatens us today is different from the massive cripplers and killers in history—like bubonic plague, cholera, or polio. Our number-one killer and our number-one health problem, the smallpox of this generation, is cardiovascular disease. It kills 500,000 people a year from heart attack and strokes, and seriously afflicts with pain and disability another 1,000,000 people each year. But unlike smallpox and similar dread diseases, cardiovascular disease, certain cancers, emphysema, and adult-onset diabetes are products of the risks incurred by living in the industrialized twentieth century. The inoculation we need for protection against these diseases is not the prick of a needle but rather a change in our thinking.

What happens to our high-tech packaging – our bodies – as we move through life is the result of our habits, the bits and pieces of our life style. We are what we do; we become what we have done. We become ill and die of the conditions brought on by our style of living.

Freud said the ultimate purpose of life was to love and to work. I will augment his idea a little. One also needs to be in good health. When you have love, work, and health, you have made a place for yourself in the world and you enhance the world.

Maintaining good health while pursuing love and work is the task of the wise man and woman. The goal is to be and remain optimally healthy for as long as possible, and to exit gracefully.

A longer span of good health, followed by a brief period of illness at the end of a full life is termed "compressed morbidity." A blessing we should all hope for is to live out our allotted life span in peace, freedom, dignity, and health. If you become ill, your quality of life is reduced, your productivity is limited. Anyone whose hair is turning gray knows that health, as a personal commodity, grows in value with age.

Priceless as good health is, it is paradoxically freely available to us, if we live the right way. The child does not have to be taught to play, but the adult must learn how to exercise. Many of us on the road to adulthood lose that childhood instinct to run and jump, to skip with joy, to walk briskly through the leaves. But it is movement, in assorted styles and speeds, on a regular basis, that is critical to maintaining our high-tech machinery.

In the recent past, more exercise was available to our bodies through daily living tasks. Before automobiles and elevators, we walked more. Our grandparents chopped wood and pitched hay. Even housewives kneading dough for bread or leaning over their washboards scrubbing clothes were "exercising." Today, exercise is something that must be superimposed onto ordinary living.

Exercise provides eight benefits to health. It takes a bit of time, but the benefits are worth it. They are: improved cardiovascular health; weight control; reduced serum cholesterol; lowered blood sugar; lowered blood pressure; increased bone density; psychological enhancement; and time held back.

Of these eight, the last two are the most difficult to measure, but hold the greatest emotional reward. With faithful exercise, your sense of well-being and confidence improves. It seems that the better your self image, through weight loss and muscle toning, the better you feel about yourself. You have a sense of energy and resilience. With that comes the feeling that you're holding back time. You are vigorous and energetic; you feel that you are living more each day; and your physician tells you that, indeed, the pounds are melting away, the cholesterol and blood pressure are dropping, and your heart functions today as it did 15 years ago.

The best news is that it is never too late to start exercising. Regardless of your age or physical condition, you still have time to begin. In my own experience with patients, I have observed it's never too late and it's never too early. This book can help you begin to make those changes that will sustain your health for life.

Good scholarship happens only with the excellent participation of all involved. For their generous time, effort, and enthusiasm, I wish to thank the staff and associates of the Stanford Center for Research in Disease Prevention, the Stanford Sports Medicine Department, and the Stanford Alumni Association. Additionally, I offer my thanks to James Fries, M.D., Professor of Medicine at the Stanford School of Medicine, for his very effective expression, "compressed morbidity."

John W. Farquhar, M.D.
Professor of Medicine
Director, Stanford Center for Research in Disease Prevention

Introduction

This book offers you several successful strategies for health promotion and disease prevention that we have used at the Stanford Center for Research in Disease Prevention. These strategies are based on many years of research and are being shared here to increase *your* knowledge about the effects of physical activity on health and enhance your skills to improve your health.

The Center was formed in 1984 to encourage interdisciplinary study and research in health promotion and prevention of chronic disease, alcohol and drug abuse, and accidental injury and death. Initially founded in 1971 as the Stanford Heart Disease Prevention Program, under the direction of Dr. John W. Farquhar, the Center has focused attention on how public health or community approaches to health promotion and disease prevention can be implemented effectively. The programs that have been developed by the Center are based on research in health education, behavioral science, and health communication. They are used to help individuals favorably influence and modify personal and environmental factors in their lifestyle. These factors, which have previously been associated with increased risk and incidence of disease, include smoking cigarettes, high blood pressure, cholesterol, stress, diet, obesity, and physical inactivity.

The contributing authors from the Center and the Sports Medicine department at Stanford include specialists in cardiology, orthopedics, epidemiology, lipid biochemistry, nutrition, psychiatry, psychology, internal medicine, exercise physiology, and sports medicine. They provide you with research data to support their recommendations, they offer you assessment techniques and skills to evaluate and design your own individualized exercise program, and they are, collectively, your rooting section to cheer you on as you begin and maintain a program of safe physical activity.

The information they provide is important to anyone wishing to maintain a healthy life. Today medical science is battling major increases in chronic and degenerative illnesses such as heart disease, cancer, arthritis, and adult-onset diabetes. Research indicates that the lifestyle choices you make can significantly lower your risk of these diseases. Although there is little you can do about some risk factors such as age, sex, and family history, we all obviously have some control over factors such as cigarette smoking, diet, alcohol use, stress, and physical activity. The strategies offered by this book can help you increase your control over these areas of your life and reduce your risk of major illness.

This book is an important addition to your personal library. We hope it will persuade you to make lifestyle choices that will not only improve your well-being, but will also help you to lay the foundation for your lifelong health and fitness.

Tony Evans, Ph.D.
Stanford University, October 1987.

*O*ne of the most obvious benefits of exercise is its ability to help control body weight.

Benefits
OF EXERCISE

So many extravagant claims have been made for exercise in recent years that many people have taken it up with misplaced expectations. Finding that exercise did not (as they had hoped) change their personality, improve their thinking processes, make them quit smoking, revolutionize their sex lives, fix their constipation, regulate their sleep patterns, and bring them an indefinable "high," they may have given up — and thus deprived themselves of the very real benefits that exercise can indeed bring.

You don't need to run marathons or even 10-kilometer races to achieve these benefits. We now have ample evidence that they can be attained at levels of exercise that are well within the capacity of the average person. For example, studies of the general population have shown that more active people have a lower risk of heart attacks,

> **William L. Haskell**, *Ph.D.,*
> *is associate professor of medicine (research) at Stanford University School of Medicine, associate director of SCRDP, consultant to the President's Council on Physical Fitness, advisor to NASA, and president of the American College of Sports Medicine Foundation.*

even when their exercise consisted mostly of gardening, stair-climbing, vigorous walking, or active games and sports.

How does exercise reduce this risk? By shifting the metabolism to a higher gear (so to speak) to supply the needed energy. In the process, the body undergoes a number of changes designed to help the muscles work more efficiently, increase their capacity, and reduce fatigue. All systems which support and supply the muscles are also "revved up" to accomplish the extra work and respond by increasing their capacity and becoming more efficient. Thus exercise has a beneficial effect on the nervous system, the whole cardiovascular system, the respiratory system, and the bones, in addition to improving the rate of metabolism of fats and carbohydrates,

But "fitness" should not be confused with health. Fitness that comes from increased physical work can't "cure" diabetes, emphysema, or hypertension, and it can't promise to prevent disease. However, it can provide highly significant health benefits in a number of areas, affecting both body and mind.

Weight Control

One of the most obvious benefits of exercise is its ability to help control body weight. In fact, it is becoming more and more apparent that many people find it extraordinarily hard to control their weight without exercise.

At the simplest level, exercise enables people who are losing weight to eat a diet that provides a reasonably good nutrient intake. For example, a small-boned woman who is inactive can maintain herself on a diet of no more than 1,200 calories a day. To lose weight by diet alone, she would have to maintain caloric levels below 1,200 for considerable periods of time. Unless she had a professional level of nutritional knowledge, she would find it extremely difficult to maintain a sufficient intake of nutrients while eating so little food. Plainly, it makes sense for someone in her position to expend a few hundred additional calories in exercise so that she can eat more. In this case, an exercise regimen using up only an additional 300-400 calories a day would allow her to increase her calorie intake by 25% and still not gain weight.

Maintenance of Lean Muscle Mass

In the case of muscle mass, it really is a case of "use it or lose it." There are obvious benefits of good-quality muscles, even if we don't all require the visible, bulging ones that are a badge of substantial strength. Without good muscles, every physical action becomes more of an effort. Those whose muscles are allowed to deteriorate with age will be less well equipped to care for themselves as they get older than those whose muscle mass has been maintained by regular exercise.   As life expectancy for Americans extends into the 70s and 80s, maintaining muscle strength by regular exercise becomes more and more essential for self-reliance and quality of life.

In addition, those who acquire and maintain a good proportion of muscle mass will find it easier to control their weight, since muscle requires more calories for its normal maintenance than does fat tissue. Simply put, at the same body weight, you can eat more without gaining weight if you have a larger muscle mass.

Bone Density

The last few years have brought increasing public awareness of the dangers of osteoporosis in post-menopausal women, and the realization that exercise can play an important role in preventing it. Any activity that applies force to bone will help build or maintain it. Runners, tennis players, and weightlifters have all been shown to have greater bone density than sedentary individuals. The effect can be quite localized; for example, tennis players have greater bone density in their dominant arm.   All the aerobic activities advocated throughout this book – such as running, walking, dancing, or bicycling – help build or maintain bone.

Ideally, the exercise habit should start in childhood and the early adult years, when increased stress on the developing bones will cause more calcium to be added to them, providing reserves that will be valuable later in life when mineral loss starts to occur.

Post-menopausally, exercise has also been shown to slow the rate of calcium loss. In one study in Wisconsin, a group of elderly women who exercised three times a week for 30 minutes each session was compared with a sedentary group. The women who exercised showed a net gain in bone density of 2.3%, while the non-exercisers showed an average bone mineral loss of 3.3% over the same period.

The amount of exercise needed in order to retain bone

mineral content cannot be precisely determined, but it is clear that calcium loss is proportional to the degree of inactivity. Those who are totally confined to bed (or who are temporarily in the weight-lessness of space) will lose calcium much more rapidly than those who have even a minimal amount of weight-bearing activity. So, any exercise is better than nothing, and systematic activity can plainly be of value.

Too much of any good thing can be harmful, however, and ironically, young women who exercise to excess may bring early osteoporosis on themselves. By reducing their body fat to the level at which their menstrual periods cease, they may cause mineral loss in the bone as if they had brought early menopause upon themselves. However, levels of exercise which produce this phenomenon are far greater than any suggested by this book!

Carbohydrates and Insulin

Exercise appears to normalize the way the body processes carbohydrates.

During large-muscle exercise of moderate intensity, the body uses the glycogen stored in the muscles to provide energy. For several days after the stored glycogen is depleted, it is replaced by glucose in the blood.

While reducing the concentration of glucose in the blood, exercise also reduces the body's need for insulin. In one study, the blood of exercisers and non-exercisers was compared, right after meals, when the circulating glucose is at its height and the body increases the output of insulin to deal with that glucose. It was found that the non-exercisers required twice as much insulin as the exercisers to remove glucose from their blood.

Swimming Builds Bones, Too

*A*lthough many experts believe only weight-bearing exercise like running, aerobics, or tennis will slow calcium loss to the bone, a study by Dr. Eric S. Orwoll, a Portland, Oregon, endocrinologist, suggests that swimming can be beneficial too.

Dr. Orwoll studied 58 men over 40 who had been swimming for at least three hours a week for at least three years. All were nonsmokers who drank little alcohol, and swimming was their only sport.

The swimmers' bones had substantially more calcium than those of 78 non-exercising men in the same age group who followed the same diet. The result could be good news for people concerned about osteoporosis – especially those who must avoid weight-bearing exercises, or who just like to swim.

Does this mean that exercise can prevent diabetes? Probably not, but at the very least, it can help by controling weight; and although cast-iron evidence is still lacking, exercise may have an independent effect. For example, islanders in the South Pacific show far greater rates of diabetes when they move to a sedentary life in the cities than when they stay relatively active in rural surroundings – differences that cannot be accounted for by differences in weight or diet.

Blood Lipids

Considerable attention has been paid in recent years to the discovery that exercise affects the cholesterol balance of the blood, reducing the levels of the harmful type (low-density-lipoprotein cholesterol, or LDL) and increasing levels of the beneficial type (high-density-lipoprotein cholesterol, or HDL). Many studies have shown that athletes such as marathon runners, cross-country runners, and dedicated tennis players have much higher levels of the beneficial HDL cholesterol than others.

The main debate about exercise and its effects on cholesterol concerns the amount needed. Plainly, not everyone is going to start training for marathons in order to tune up his or her blood chemistry. However, it appears that, as with calcium, the benefits of exercise can be plotted on a continuous line. People who spend their lives in bed will have the lowest levels of HDL cholesterol and those who are most active the highest. Any activity is therefore better than none.

High Blood Pressure

The chapter on blood pressure (page 124) carries more information on the effects of exercise on blood pressure and on the various factors that can cause pressure to rise. Suffice it to say here that there is now increasing evidence that exercise can help to prevent the rise in blood pressure that the average American experiences with increasing age. There is also evidence that endurance exercise training programs decrease blood pressure in some hypertensive patients. Some of this decrease may result from the weight-reducing effects of exercise, but some of the benefit is due to a "down regulation" of the nervous system.

Psychological Benefits

This is an area for which much has been claimed. Even though many of these claims have been exaggerated, and you are not guaranteed eternal bliss with a jogging mileage of 20 or 30 miles a week, the psychological benefits are still considerable. If you have ever exercised regularly, you are aware of them. If not, it may be hard to convince you of their existence. I am not talking here of the "runner's high," or any similar sense of euphoria; people who report those feelings are usually those who exercise at a rather more intense level than we advocate in this book.

Even with moderate exercise, the psychological benefits are considerable. For example, regular exercisers (even at moderate levels) report less anxiety and depression and feel they are better able to cope with stress when they exercise than when they don't.

In spite of valiant attempts, researchers have not yet pinned down a cast-iron physiological reason for this improvement in mental state, although some have suggested that the reasons may be found in a reduction of adrenaline in the blood and an increase in the amount of endorphins, a natural tranquilizer produced by the body. However, these biological mechanisms have yet to be substantiated as the cause of improvements in the exerciser's mental state. What can be said, beyond doubt, is that exercise improves mental outlook and the ability to control stress in two ways:

• By providing a socially acceptable way to spend time away from the stresses of everyday life.
• By improving self-image and self-esteem.

Eleven studies which set out to examine the effect of aerobic exercise on self-esteem found positive results, which is not surprising. Exercise gives you the feeling that you have accomplished something worthwhile, and at the same time can make you look and feel younger.

Aging

More than anything else that has yet been invented, exercise can help to hold back time. It really can make us physiologically younger than our sedentary contemporaries.

If you take various measures of body function and structure, and compare exercisers in their 50s and 60s with sedentary people of the same age, you will find that the exercisers are physiologically 10 to 20 years younger. Their cardiovascular function, their body composition, their blood lipids, and their appearance are all in significantly better condition than those of their contemporaries who are growing old in rocking chairs.

And if that isn't enough, you can be sure that the exercisers get more enjoyment out of life!

Eight Benefits of Exercise

1. **It improves cardiovascular health.**
2. **It is a key to weight control.**
3. **It improves blood fat and cholesterol profiles.**
4. **It lowers blood sugar.**
5. **It helps lower blood pressure.**
6. **It maintains and increases bone density.**
7. **It provides psychological benefits.**
8. **It holds back time.**

All parts of the body which have a function, if used in moderation and exercised in labours in which each is accustomed, become thereby healthy, well developed and age more slowly; but if unused and left idle they become liable to disease, defective in growth and age quickly. Hippocrates

Exercise

Despite Mark Twain's pronouncement, "The only exercise I get is being a pallbearer for my more active friends," writers, philosophers, and scientists have celebrated the benefits of regular exercise for a long time. During the twentieth century, especially, we have made great strides in understanding what actually happens to the body during exercise and physical activity and also how it contributes to physical fitness and health.

Exercise Defined

Let's start by considering the definitions of terms that frequently are used interchangeably but are actually different concepts, i.e. *physical activity, exercise,* and *physical fitness.*.

Physical activity has been defined as any bodily movement produced by the skeletal muscles resulting in energy expenditure that can be measured in kilocalories. Such activities can be categorized into:

- occupational
- recreational or leisure-time
- sports
- conditioning
- and household activities.

Exercise is a part of physical activity but is distinct because it is planned, structured, and repetitive (see following figure).

Physical fitness is a combination of attributes associated

Tony Evans, Ph.D., is a research associate in the SCRDP and the Division of Cardiology, Stanford University School of Medicine, and project director of a National Institutes of Health funded Physical Activity Measurement Study.

Probability that phyical activity performed during selected catagories is exercise

Sleep

Occupation

Leisure
  Conditioning

Sports

Household

Other

Zero or low   High

Source: *Public Health Reports* 100:126-146, March-April 1985

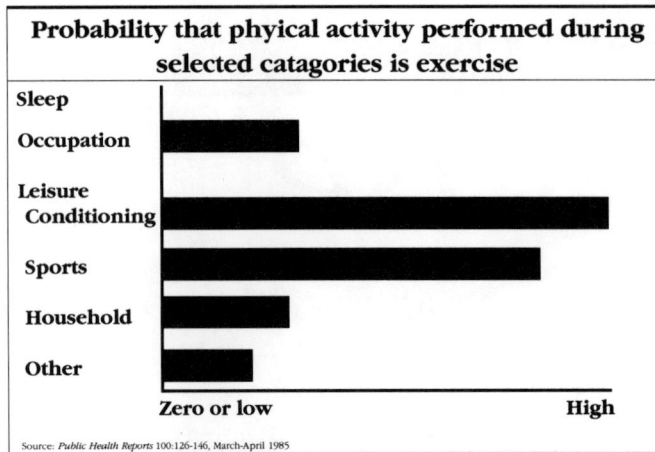

with the development of physical skills, such as speed and agility, or health-related issues such as strength, flexibility, endurance, and body composition.

The components of physical fitness programs that are important for the optimal development of health and performance are summarized in the following figure. In this chapter we will look at how physical activity and exercise can be effectively combined to enhance health-related fitness.

Muscular Strength and Endurance

Components of physical fitness

Physical fitness

  Health-related fitness
    Cardiorespiratory endurance
    Muscular strength
    Body composition
    Flexibility

  skill-related fitness
    Agility
    Balance
    Coordination
    Speed
    Power
    Reaction time

Source: *Public Health Reports* 100:126-146, March-April 1985

Muscle strength and endurance, although quite separate components of fitness, are highly related in many activities. The strength of a muscle is its capacity to exert force through contraction of muscle fibers. Since the force that a muscle exerts is directly related to its size, those individuals with large muscles have the potential to develop a lot of strength and exert large amounts of force. Differences in strength between individuals and between the sexes can be partially explained by factors including amount of muscle tissue, amount of sex hormones (primarily the male hormone testosterone), and social or cultural influences.

Strength is an important fitness component, but the optimal amount varies with individual needs and occupations.

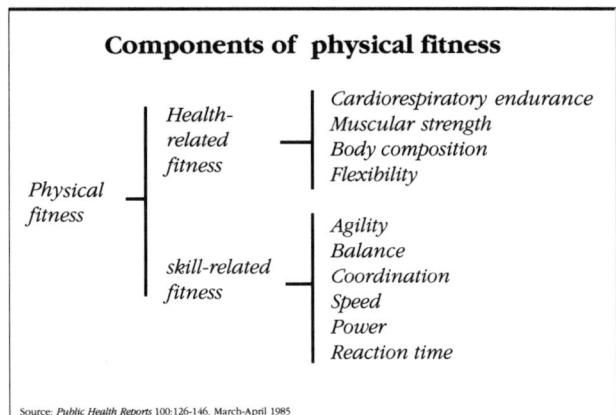

Fire fighters and construction workers, for example, have strength needs that are quite different from those of a person who works at a desk all day. Athletes have other strength requirements that are specific to the demands of their sport. Physically demanding occupations and sports require certain levels of strength development for safe participation.

Muscular endurance refers to the ability of any muscle group to repeat muscle contractions against resistance over a period of time. It can also be measured as the amount of time one can sustain a specific muscle contraction. For example, endurance can be measured by the number of times we can successfully maneuver each mogul on the ski slope before becoming tired, or how long we can hold the tuck position on an exhilarating downhill schuss.

Muscles develop endurance as they develop mechanisms to accommodate the increased metabolic demands placed on them. Repeated muscular contractions stimulate an increased blood flow to the muscle, providing the extra oxygen, nutrients, and enzymes necessary for the muscle to continue to work and postpone fatigue.

Types of Exercise

Muscular strength and endurance can be developed by using static *isometric contractions* and dynamic *isotonic* and *isokinetic* muscle contractions. Isometric contractions were popularized by Charles Atlas in the 1950s in his "dynamic tension" program. The strip cartoons that advertised the program suggested that static exercises could result in significant muscular development. Since the early '50s, numerous research studies have reported the effects of isometric exercise on strength development. These studies indicated that strength could be increased with isometric exercises, but not to the extent previously claimed.

An example of an isometric contraction would be to simply contract the quadricep muscle of the thigh with the knee extended, not moving the hip or knee joint. To achieve the best results in isometric strength development, maximum contractions must be held for at least six seconds several times per day. The greatest disadvantage of isometrics appears to be that strength is developed only at the angle at which the contraction is held. In order to gain strength through the full range of movement using this technique, a muscle group would have to undergo numerous six-second contractions at various angles in its normal range of movement.

Isometric or static exercises should be used cautiously in exercise programs for older adults or for those who have, or are suspected to have, coronary heart disease. This type of exercise causes a reflex acceleration of the heart, while at the same time restricting venous blood flow to the heart. As a result, isometric exercise can cause an unusually high increase in blood pressure relative to heart rate and a possible reduction in oxygen supply to the heart.

Isotonic Contractions

More universally valuable in developing strength are isotonic contractions, the type we use when we engage in such activities as lifting a box to move it from one table to another. An isotonic workout involves placing weight at a given distance from the joint axis of rotation and lifting it. When the weight is at its greatest perpendicular distance from the axis of rotation, the muscle is worked to its maximum capacity.

Effective strength-training programs using isotonic techniques usually apply the "progressive resistance exercise" and "overload" principles. In the progressive resistance approach, the exerciser works with a specific weight until it can be lifted for several repetitions. Further strength gains are made by adding small increments of additional weight or resistance. Strength improvement using the overload concept results from muscles being loaded beyond their normal capacity.

Greek mythology illustrates both these principles in the story of Milo of Crotona, who set about becoming the strongest man in the world by lifting a young bull each day until the bull was full grown. How times have changed. These days, most people eat the meat instead of lifting it and develop atherosclerosis and heart disease instead of strength and physical fitness!

Instead of bulls, isotonic exercisers today can make use of a diverse range of equipment. However, traditional barbells or free weights are still the favorite equipment for serious strength-training aficionados. Novices to weight-training exercise are probably best served by the convenience and safety of training facilities that utilize equipment such as Universal and Nautilus machines.

Strength development using isotonic contractions is limited by the constant level of resistance throughout the movement. The amount of weight lifted is thus limited to the maximum that can be lifted at the weakest point in the muscle group's range of contraction.

Isokinetic Contractions

Isokinetic contractions effectively address the limitations of strength development associated with both isotonic and isometric contractions. In an isokinetic contraction, the speed of the contraction remains constant, but the resistance offered by the machine matches the individual's capability throughout the range of motion. This is referred to as "accommodating resistance" and permits a maximum contraction to be performed through a full range of movement.

The isokinetic contraction was first introduced in 1968 by a bioengineer, James Perrine, who developed a speed-controlled dynamometer called a Cybex machine. Numerous other devices have now been developed that provide a similar type of variable resistance. The Keiser K300, Nautilus, Hydrafitness, the CES system, Isopower 5000, and Kin-Com are just a few of the latest pieces of equipment that utilize principles of muscle contraction similar to those first developed by Perrine. The cost of this type of equipment is usually prohibitive for individual purchase, and it is usually found in health clubs and rehabilitation settings.

Isotonic or isokinetic equipment can be used to develop both muscle strength and endurance. However, exercise programs that are designed to develop strength or endurance vary in the relationship between the amount of resistance and number of repetitions. If strength is the main requirement, the number of repetitions for an exercise is kept low and the resistance is high. In a muscular endurance program, the repetitions are high and the resistance is low.

Cardiovascular Endurance

Cardiovascular endurance includes stamina, aerobic fitness, aerobic capacity, and functional capacity. Although aerobic fitness is the current "in" term used to describe cardiovascular endurance, *functional capacity* or *maximal oxygen consumption* (VO_2max) is the accepted universal terminology.

The ability to exercise continuously for short or long periods of time depends upon how effectively the heart, lungs, arteries, capillaries, cells, and veins can transfer oxygen, carbon dioxide, nutrients and waste products to and from the working muscles. As soon as an individual starts to exercise, the body adapts to the increased energy demands being placed on it. Energy stores of glycogen are mobilized within the muscles to provide the fuel necessary for them to contract. At the same time, since the muscles also need more oxygen, the heart and respiration rates increase to provide more oxygenated blood.

As long as the working muscles can receive an adequate amount of oxygen to continue a process called oxidation in the muscle cells, exercise can continue and fatigue is offset. This type of exercise is frequently referred to as *aerobic exercise*. When the working muscles build up waste products such as lactic acid at a rate that outstrips the supply of oxygen to the muscle cells, this is referred to as *anaerobic exercise*, and fatigue results in a short period of time.

Oxygen supply for the muscles depends on a healthy heart, which must make more oxygen available to the muscles by increasing its rate of contraction during exercise. As heart rate increases, more blood circulates each minute, thereby increasing the cardiac output of the heart. Direct measurement of cardiac output is a complicated procedure done primarily in a laboratory setting. Fortunately, it can be measured indirectly by determining a person's VO_2 max, or the amount of oxygen the body is able to use per minute when exercising maximally during a medically supervised exercise test. Simply stated, if cardiac output increases, so does maximal oxygen consumption.

Further, since maximal oxygen consumption depends upon an efficient respiratory system, the measurement of maximal oxygen consumption is one of the best measurements of dynamic heart and lung function available. Another term that is frequently used in place of maximal oxygen consumption is functional capacity, measured in milliliters of oxygen per kilogram of body weight per minute (ml/kg/min).

Age, sex, genetics, and lifestyle result in a wide variation among the population regarding this fitness measure. As the graph on page 24 shows, people who lead active lifestyles, independent of age, have higher VO_2 max values than their sedentary counterparts.

Cardiovascular endurance can be developed by a training program based on variations of the "F.I.T." principle: that is, with the *Frequency*, *Intensity*, and *Training* duration necessary to produce physiological changes over a period of time. These may include changes in:

- resting heart rate and blood pressure, submaximal exercise heart rate, and blood pressure and body weight
- body composition (the percentages of the body that are muscle, bone, and connective tissues by comparison with body fat)
- lipoproteins (chemical structures present in the blood that carry fat, proteins and cholesterol)
- fat and carbohydrate metabolism (the way the body utilizes fat and sugar carried in blood)
- and bone mineralization.

Accompanying psychological changes may include a reduction in stress, depression, and anxiety, and an improvement in self-image.

The training intensity necessary to produce such physiological and psychological change is not constant. It varies from one individual to another and is different for people of different ages, sex, and health status.   However, if you select the appropriate type of exercise for your current level of fitness and set it at the proper intensity, duration, and frequency, then improvements in physical fitness and associated health benefits should occur. The exercise program should follow three basic principles of exercise training: overload (doing more than was done previously), specificity (relating the activity to your specific needs), and progression (starting out slowly and adding small increments of time and/or distance as fitness improves).

The table on the following page from the March-April 1985 *Public Health Reports* offers guidelines to improve health and fitness for people in different age groups.

Differences in maximal oxygen consumption between active and sedentary individuals

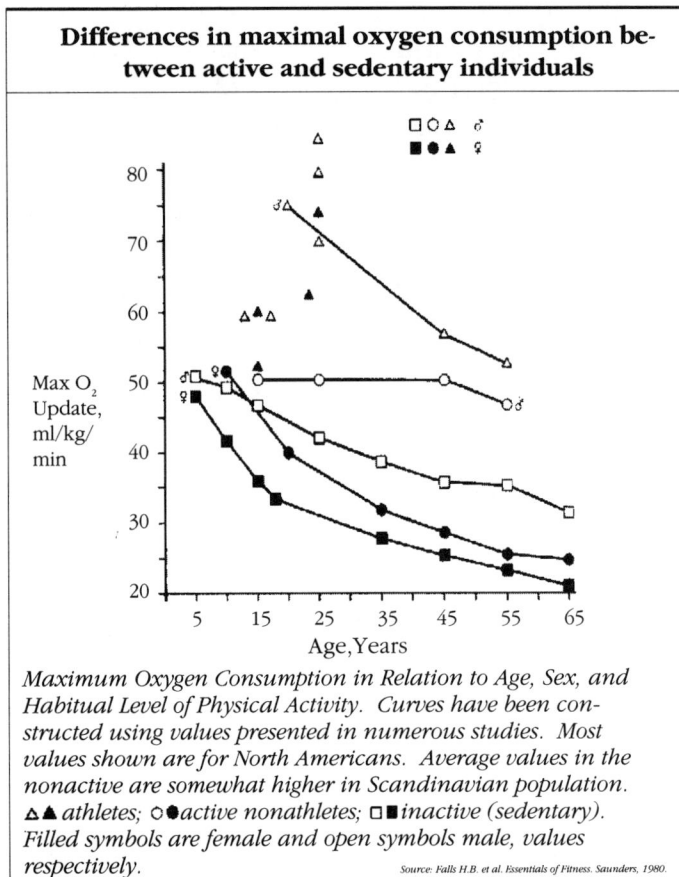

Max O$_2$ Update, ml/kg/min

Maximum Oxygen Consumption in Relation to Age, Sex, and Habitual Level of Physical Activity. Curves have been constructed using values presented in numerous studies. Most values shown are for North Americans. Average values in the nonactive are somewhat higher in Scandinavian population. △▲ athletes; ○● active nonathletes; □■ inactive (sedentary). Filled symbols are female and open symbols male, values respectively.

Source: Falls H.B. et al. Essentials of Fitness. Saunders, 1980.

You may find that many fitness books and magazines recommend an exercise intensity in a target heart rate zone of 70-85% of your age-predicted maximum heart rate. This is high intensity exercise for the majority of the population. Maximum heart rate (MHR) can be determined by using the simple formula:

MHR = 220-age (low estimate) or 210-(.5 x age) (high estimate).

A physical activity plan for improving health and fitness in specific age groups.

Major health-fitness goals	Physical activity plan[1]

Youth (1 - 14 years)

- Optimal physical growth and development
- Good psychological adjustment
- Develop interest and skills for active lifestyle as adult
- Reduction of CHD[2] risk factors

T Emphasis on large muscle, dynamic exercise; moving body over distance and against gravity; some heavy resistive activity and flexibility exercise
I Moderate to vigorous intensity
D Total of more than 30 minutes per day in 1 or more sessions
F Every day
G Increased activity to and from school

Young adults (15 - 24 years)

- Optimal physical growth and development
- Good psychological adjustment
- Reduction of CHD risk factors
- Develop interest and skills for active lifestyle as adult

T Emphasis on large muscle, dynamic strength and flexibility exercise
I Moderate to vigorous intensity (more than 50 percent VO_2Max)
D Total of more than 30 minutes per session (more than 4 kilocalories per Kg of body weight)
F At least every other day
G Increased activity to and from school

Adults (25-65 years)

- Prevention and treatment of CHD
- Prevention and treatment of Type II diabetes
- Maintenance of optimal body composition
- Enhance psychological status
- Retain musculoskeletal integrity

T Emphasis on large muscle dynamic exercise; some heavy resistive and flexibility exercises
I Moderate intensity (more than 50 percent VO_2Max)
D Total of more than 30 minutes per session (more than 4 kilocalories per Kg of body weight)
F At least every other day
G Lower level activities (e.g. walking) every day

Older adults (over 65 years)

- Maintain general functional capacity
- Retain musculoskeletal integrity
- Enhance psychological status
- Prevent and treat CHD and Type II diabetes

T Emphasis on moving about, flexibility, and some resistive exercises
I Moderate intensity (overload with slow progression)
D Based on capacity of individual, up to 60 minutes per day in multiple sessions
F Every day
G Lower level activities (for example, walking) every day

---

[1]Key: T = Type of Exercise
  I = Intensity
  D = Duration or amount
  F = Frequency of exercise session
  G = Goal

[2]Coronary Heart Disease

However, the problem with using this method to set your exercise training level is that it uses an estimation of your maximum heart rate based on population averages. It is important to recognize this particular limitation and adjust your training heart rate accordingly. It is critical from an adherence and injury-prevention perspective not to set this training heart rate too high. Several research studies have now shown that fitness gains, as well as beneficial health effects, can be obtained with training programs that utilize low and moderate intensity exercise.

A variety of training programs exist to develop cardiovascular endurance. Essentially, they consist of or combine the following methods:

- interval training (exercise and rest intervals are organized in various combinations)
- continuous training (exercise intensity is adjusted to permit long bouts of continuous exercise)
- interval-circuit training (running, walking, and calisthenic exercise is incorporated into a circuit that can vary in distance and time).

Flexibility

Many individuals become aware of flexibility, or the range of movement of limbs around a joint, only as they get older or if they participate in activities where its presence or absence clearly affects their physical performance. Flexibility is a component of fitness that one is acutely aware of following an injury such as a fractured limb, where for a period of time limb immobilization is required or normal movement is limited. These periods of immobilization serve as an excellent example of how inactivity affects the body. Muscle size and strength are reduced considerably as the muscle atrophies. Range of movement of the limb is also severely compromised. After the cast is removed, a rehabilitation program is begun to help the injured body part resume its previous function. Initially, strength and flexibility exercises are an important part of the rehabilitation program.

Flexibility exercises are useful because they increase the range of motion of a joint, allowing muscles to exert strength (force) for a longer period of time. This is particularly noticeable in activities like swimming, gymnastics, and golf, where increased flexibility in the wrist, elbow, and shoulder joints can enhance performance. Usually, people who have adequate flexibility are less likely to incur injuries.

Chronic low back problems, a major cause of disability in the U.S., have been recognized in clinical settings to be related to various structural problems, including poor abdominal strength and inflexibility in the muscles of the low back and thigh (hamstrings).

Flexibility exercises have usually been recommended as part of the warm-up period that precedes exercise. However, there is not uniform agreement among researchers regarding the beneficial effects of flexibility exercises done prior to exercise. Some suggest that some light form of aerobic activity such as walking or slow jogging is important to provide sufficient "warm up" of the skeletal muscular system prior to initiating stretching or flexibility exercises. The increased body temperature increases the circulatory supply to the skeletal muscular system and thus prepares both muscles and joints for efficient stretching and activity.

A variety of flexibility exercises have been developed for use in exercise programs in home, medical, and professional environments. They all basically fit into one of two categories: *static* or *ballistic* stretches.

In static stretching, the body part being exercised is stretched lightly to lengthen the muscle, and the stretched position is then held for a period of 20 - 30 seconds. Slow breathing can enhance relaxation during this stretch. During the period of stretch the length of the muscle will slowly increase, thus ensuring an optimal length over which the muscle will be able to contract during subsequent exercise.

Ballistic stretches are of several types, all of which involve visible movement. The typical ballistic stretch is one that uses the momentum of body weight to induce the stretch. This form of "bouncy" or "jerky" stretching is not recommended, since it can compromise certain reflex mechanisms in the muscles and tendons surrounding the joint and may result in injury.

Ballistic stretches that incorporate slow movements have been used for many years by dancers and those who practice yoga. The stretch is done in a slow and controlled manner throughout the range of movement of the specific activity to be performed. Since the stretch is controlled, there is a minimal risk of injury to the muscle or joint.

A more recent approach to flexibility exercise is called *proprioceptive neuromuscular facilitation* (PNF). In this method of muscle and joint stretching, the muscle is first tightened (contracted) and then statically stretched. Although flexibility can be achieved by this method, residual muscle soreness has also been reported. This method also requires a partner and is more time-consuming to perform than the other methods.

Among the flexibility methods, the static method appears to be the safest as well as most practical and effective for the majority of individuals interested in participating in a regular exercise program.

Flexibility varies among different joints in the body. It is dependent on the structure and the function of the joint. The shoulder and knee joints, for example, are structurally very different. The shoulder joint is a much more flexible joint, with a greater range of motion, than the knee. The range of motion of a joint is influenced by structures that surround it, such as muscle, ligaments, and tendons. In order to prevent injury, it is important to ensure that an appropriate balance between strength and flexibility be established around joints. Excessive range of motion in a joint or an imbalance in strength of muscles surrounding a joint can result in injury.

Body Composition

Body composition is the term used to describe the proportions of muscle, fat, bone, and other connective tissues in the body. These various body tissues are classified further to describe lean body weight (LBW) and fat weight (FW). It is possible to determine the relative percentage of total body weight that is composed of LBW and FW by using a variety of assessment techniques.

The only accurate way to measure body composition directly is to dissect the body and literally weigh each of its various tissue components. Not very practical for those interested in participating in exercise after the assessment has been completed! Other popular techniques that have been used in the past to estimate body composition include skin-fold and girth measurements. Recent technological advances have resulted in some attempts to use nuclear magnetic resonance and bioelectrical impedance. However, the most widely used and accurate indirect assessment method to determine body composition is *hydrostatic weighing*. This method determines body density (body density = body weight/body volume) by weighing a person on an accurate scale in air, then weighing the person submerged in water after he or she has expired as much air as possible from the lungs. Appropriate corrections and calculations are made to this information, and the result is a determination of lean body weight and fat weight as a percentage of total body weight.

What is the ideal body weight and composition that is associated with optimal health, and how can we achieve it? Research suggests that men and women have ideal body weight when their percentage of body fat is, respectively, 15 - 18% and 22 - 25% of total body weight. However, it is important to remember that individual variation other than sex, such as age and physical activity level, can result in changes in these percentages.

Although body build (the genetic contribution to our form and structure) and body size (height and mass) can only be changed minimally by a regular exercise program, significant changes can occur in body composition. As a population, the changes in body composition are illustrated in a decrease in muscle mass and an increase in body fat and total body weight as we get older. Although this is the norm for the majority of the American population, there is also substantial evidence that indicates these changes in body composition are not mandatory.

ACTIVITIES THAT RATE HIGH IN CARDIOVASCULAR-RESPIRATORY BENEFITS AND THEIR APPROXIMATE ENERGY EXPENDITURES.

Summarized are some of the better cardiovascular-respiratory exercises and the number of Kcal expended per hour of the exercise. An important concept is to select several of these activities that are enjoyable, and to use them in such a way that scheduled exercise sessions are looked forward to, not dreaded.

Caloric consumption is based on a 150 lb. person. There is a 10% increase in caloric consumption for each 15 lbs. over this weight and 10% decrease for each 15 lbs. under.

ACTIVITY	KCAL PER HOUR
Badminton, competitive singles	480
Basketball	360-660
Bicycling	
10 mph	420
11 mph	480
12 mph	600
Calisthenics, heavy	600
Handball, competitive	660
Rope skipping, vigorous	800
Rowing machine	840
Running	
5 mph	600
6 mph	750
7 mph	870
8 mph	1,020
9 mph	1,130
Skating, ice or roller, rapid	700
Skiing, downhill, vigorous	600
Skiing, cross-country	
2.5 mph	560
4 mph	600
8 mph	1,020
Swimming, 25-50 yards per min.	360-750
Walking	
Level road, 4 mph (fast)	420
Upstairs	600-1,080
Uphill, 3.5 mph	480-900
Gardening, much lifting, stooping, digging	500
Mowing, pushing handmower	450
Sawing hardwwod	600
Shoveling, heavy	660
Wood chopping	560

SOURCE: Wynder EL. The Book of Health: The American Health Foundation. New York: Franklin Watts, Inc., 1981. Used with permission.

People who maintain an active lifestyle which includes regular physical activity using the large muscle groups in the body are able to maintain optimal body weight and body composition. Regular exercise increases lean body weight and decreases fat weight. This is doubly desirable because muscle mass is more active metabolically than fat, i.e., it has greater energy needs than fat (which is primarily a storage facility for energy). Increasing muscle mass is like increasing engine capacity. With a larger engine, we use more fuel, and since most of the fuel is stored in fat, we are able to effectively reduce our fat stores and favorably affect our body composition.

Effective weight and body composition control involves both caloric expenditure (exercise) as well as caloric restriction (diet). The relative merits of both methods of controlling body weight and composition have received substantial research attention in the past (see the chapter on "Diet and Exercise" for more information). In 1985, a National Institutes of Health consensus panel on obesity underscored the importance of optimal body composition by indicating that losing weight is not just a matter of vanity, it is a matter of health.

Physical fitness is important to the development of optimal health. It helps us avoid the significant negative physiological and psychological effects on health that results from inactivity and deconditioning.

Muscular strength and endurance, cardiovascular endurance, flexibility, and body composition all have an impact on physical fitness and health. Understanding the effects of exercise and physical activity on each of these is important if we are to experience the health benefits of exercise and avoid the health risks.

Myth: Eating protein builds muscles.
Fact: Use of muscles — not intake of excessive protein — is what builds muscles.

Myths

*I*n spite of all that has been written about exercise in the last decade, there is still widespread confusion regarding its risks and benefits. Part of this confusion is due to exercise myths that influence our behaviors.

Myths rise out of fads, folklore, and fantasy. They originate from our individual wishes, from Madison Avenue-created fashions, and from the collective cultural beliefs about exercise, health, and fitness. You can exercise for fitness and for pleasure, and you can do it safely, when facts protect you from the claims and aims of others.

> **Tia Rich**, M.A., is assistant director of the Stanford University Health Improvement Program, and instructor in the Stanford Executive Program and Sloan Fellow Program of the Stanford Graduate School of Business.

Why We Don't Exercise

MYTH:

If you are physically tired by your exertions at the end of the day, you probably had enough exercise.

FACT:

You are getting enough exercise only if you do rhythmic, continuous movement at least three days a week to reach and sustain your target heart rate for 20 minutes or more.

MYTH:

You need to be athletic to exercise.

FACT:

There are many excellent, brisk activities which do not require any special athletic abilities. In fact, many people who find competitive sports difficult have discovered that there are other activities that are easy to do and enjoyable.

No matter what your body type, background, or ability, there is an activity waiting for you. Know your body and what type of movement it is suited for. Using your body in activities for which you have a natural inclination will enhance your enjoyment of the movements.

MYTH:

Exercise is stressful and does not lead to relaxation.

FACT:

Exercise can be just the activity to help you relax..

Exercise is stressful only if you push yourself too hard, too fast, or if you occasionally exercise intensely but are sedentary most of the time. Pace yourself. By building up your program gradually, you may find exercise relieves stress, lifts depression, helps you think more clearly and improves sleep. Many people feel energized, refreshed, and relaxed after exercising.

MYTH:

Regular exercise takes many hours every week.

FACT:

Regular exercise does not have to take more than 20 - 30 minutes, three days a week. Once you have established a comfortable exercise routine, exercising becomes a natural part of your life.

Including exercise in your regular schedule might require a little more organization, but this does not have to be an insurmountable obstacle. Here are helpful tips for creating time for exercise:

- Time it so the post-workout shower becomes your regular shower.
- Keep your exercise clothes in your car or office.

- Get together with a group of other people with young children and share the babysitting.
- Take a walk with a friend instead of having a drink or meal together.

MYTH:

Exercise is risky business — Jim Fixx died while running.

FACT:

Jim Fixx, author of the 1977 bestseller The Complete Book of Running, *died during a run not because of his running, but because he had heart disease. Running could not make him invulnerable to his heredity (his father died of a heart attack at age 43; Jim was 52 at his death) or his past lifestyle which had included significant stress, cigarette smoking, and obesity.*

How We Exercise

MYTH:

No pain, no gain.

FACT:

Train! Don't strain.

Muscle pain or soreness during exercise is your body's way of telling you that something is wrong. It occurs when metabolic wastes – especially lactic acid – build up. This can be avoided so long as the working muscles receive adequate oxygen with which to dissipate the waste products.

Pain and soreness are signals to slow down, ease up, and work within the healthy "training" capacity of your body. You can expand your capacity by gradually increasing your physical activity. If you keep going until you get a burning sensation, you'll be more susceptible to injury. Your body has its own wisdom. Learn to listen to it. It is your best coach.

MYTH:
The more exercise the better.
FACT:
As with most things in life, too much exercise can be harmful. Exercising can be taken to extremes and become a compulsion, which can lead to unhealthy effects.

It is smart to limit your exertion from the outset. Planning your exercise prudently before you start will help you avoid getting into a situation where you suspect you should stop but don't, due to social pressures and competition. In the heat of the activity, when your own enthusiasm or others' eggs you on, risk may seem remote. Aches, pains, and heavy breathing which could be warning signs are all too easy to dismiss in the pleasures and striving of the moment.

By ignoring such symptoms, you could be courting catastrophe. In the studies and reports of exercise injuries and deaths, denial of warning symptoms is a recurring theme. Experienced athletes and novices alike are guilty of such denial, and they are equally likely to suffer from it.

Unless you are a competitive athlete in a controlled training program, you could subject yourself to injury if you exercise to your limits, even if you have no symptoms. Remain on the side of safety and use your pulse to guide you (see page 73 for the appropriate heart rates).

MYTH:
Exercising in the morning is best.
FACT:
Any time of day is a good time to exercise!

Listen to your body and you will discover your own best time to exercise, determined by your need for exhilaration, stress reduction, relaxation or enhanced concentration. The morning has the advantage of invigorating crispness. The golden hour of sunset can provide a refreshing transition from work to home. Decide for yourself which time of day best meets your needs.

Exercise and Health

MYTH:

Exercise prolongs life.

FACT:

This continues to be a controversial area of research.

Longitudinal studies by Dr. Ralph Paffenbarger of Stanford have shown that people with more active lifestyles have a reduced risk of premature death from coronary heart disease and may increase their lifespan (see the chapter "Exercise and Long Life"). Research on this topic continues.

In the short term, however, it's important to recognize the positive effects of exercise on the quality of your daily life. Enjoy the benefits of exercise you are reaping today.

MYTH:

Habitual exercise helps the immune system.

FACT:

Many regular exercisers do notice a decrease in infections, but the exerciser's total lifestyle, which includes healthier diet choices and a reduction in stress levels, smoking and weight, could contribute to the reported decrease in infections.

In a review of the immunology of exercise, Dr. Harvey B. Simon (*Journal of the American Medical Association*, November 16, 1984) concluded that exercise does produce a transient increase in white blood cells which are the body's main line of defense against infections.

It is interesting to note that industrial fitness programs lead to decreased absenteeism. But further research is needed to determine the effect of exercise on the immune system.

MYTH:

Exercise reduces cholesterol.

FACT:

*Many researchers are affirming that exercise may increase the level of "good" cholesterol, (high-density lipoprotein or HDL) in the blood. These researchers also have found, however, that exercise does not significantly lower **total** serum cholesterol. A low-fat, low-cholesterol diet along with exercise is the best way to reduce total serum cholesterol.*

A diet high in carbohydrates (rice, whole-grain bread, pasta) and low in fat and cholesterol is beneficial for everyone, whether sedentary or active. It is important to acknowledge that on an individual basis people can do all the right things and still have high cholesterol, and people can do all the wrong things and have low cholesterol. All one can say is that 10,000 people doing all the right things will have lower cholesterol levels than will 10,000 people all doing the wrong things. Consistently, data shows that active people have fewer diseases and that the diseases they have are less severe. The best bet is to live prudently — eat a low-fat, low-cholesterol diet, exercise, manage your weight and stress, refrain from smoking — and hope you are one of those for whom prudent living pays off.

MYTH:

Exercise prevents heart attacks.

FACT:

Exercise does not make you impervious to coronary illness.

This myth is rooted in a "myth of invulnerability." In the words of Dr. Kenneth Cooper, founder and president of the Cooper Clinic and Aerobics Center in Dallas:

"It is important to acknowledge that there is absolutely nothing known to man that is totally protective against coronary heart disease, whether it is medicine, surgery, or marathon running. Furthermore, the heart is masterful at disguising its problems. You can run along for miles and miles at a heart rate of 150 to 160 beats per minute. You may feel quite energetic, and you certainly may not experience any pain. But even as you run, you could be suffering from undiagnosed arteriosclerosis (occlusion of the arteries)."

Jim Fixx is an example of the fact that a person can exercise without any symptoms of heart disease and suffer the tragedy of sudden death if the whole picture of all the risk factors associated with heart disease is ignored. Whatever your fitness level, heredity, high blood pressure, high cholesterol, obesity, and smoking all need to be kept in mind when assessing your health.

Depending on your medical history and risk factors, it may be important to use a medically supervised exercise treadmill test to assess the health of your cardiovascular system and to discuss your exercise plans with your doctor before beginning an exercise program.

MYTH:
Resting heart rate is a reliable measure of fitness.
FACT:

"The heart rate varies widely from individual to individual and also within the same individual from one observation to another under similar circumstances; therefore it is almost meaningless to speak of a normal heart rate. Resting heart rate is affected by so many variables that it has very little meaning for the prediction of physical performance. (Herbert A. Devries, Physiology of Exercise: For Physical Education and Athletics).

The average resting heart rate in an adult male standing up is approximately 70 - 80 beats per minute. It averages five to ten beats faster in females and can be 10-12 beats faster when standing up as opposed to lying down. Following are some of the factors that affect the resting heart rate.

- Eating a meal.
- Emotional stress.
- A rise in body temperature above normal.
- Hot temperatures, humidity, and lack of air movement.
- Smoking and caffeine.

Exercise and Weight

MYTH:

It's dangerous to exercise if you are overweight.

FACT:

Exercise is an essential component of healthy weight management.

Exercise helps you burn more calories and thus helps you manage your weight. There is also some evidence that you will burn more calories during the hours following exercise (see the chapter "Diet and Exercise"). Low-impact exercises, such as walking or cycling, with their reduced risk of injury, are excellent for helping you lose weight and keep it off.

MYTH:

Spot reduction works: A person can reduce fat in specific parts of the body with toning exercises.

FACT:

Reports of successful spot reduction from exercises such as bent- knee curl-ups are based on the reduction of girth that results from the increased strength and tone of the exercised muscles. Fat deposits, however, cannot be especially reduced by "spot exercising" the muscles directly beneath them.

Fat deposits can be reduced only by aerobic exercise, and then they are reduced proportionately from all fat stores in the body. Toning exercises have their aesthetic merits but don't lead to local fat reduction.

Dr. James S. Skinner, Ph.D., Director of the Exercise and

Sports Research Institute at Arizona State University, states: "Time and time again it has been shown that there is no such thing as spot reducing. You're born with a profile, and you put on fat in certain places according to some individual pattern and your sex. Every 14 days all the fat in cells has turned over. If you start turning over more by losing weight, your body loses fat proportionately all over. You may lose more in absolute terms in certain areas, but you don't selectively lose fat in those areas."

MYTH:
Exercise significantly increases appetite and is not beneficial for weight loss.

FACT:
Increased activity brings about increased caloric need, so it is possible to eat more and weigh less if you exercise.

Research done at Stanford on exercisers and non-exercisers has shown that those who exercise regularly have a higher caloric intake while at the same time having lower weight and body fat. Thus, exercise does increase appetite but exercisers actually manage their weight better than people who diet. Exercise also may enhance your enjoyment of eating by heightening your sensory and mental clarity so your can more keenly experience the sensation of hunger and the pleasure of eating.

MYTH:
You can exercise away your "cellulite."

FACT:
Fat is fat! There is no unique entity known as "cellulite."

The term "cellulite" was invented by a French beauty shop owner. However, the *Journal of the American Medical Association* reports, "There is no medical condition known as cellulite." "Cellulite" is just plain fat that has accumulated near the surface of the skin. Special treatments such as massage, creams, brushes, lotions, rubber pants, and therapies at cellulite salons do not break down fat.

MYTH:

Wearing special clothing such as rubberized suits or heavy sweatsuits will help you lose weight.

FACT:

Excess sweating does not equal more weight loss. The weight loss from profuse sweating is water loss (not fat) and therefore only temporary.

Nonporous and heavy sweatsuits enclose the body in a hot environment, preventing the evaporation of sweat necessary to cool the body during heavy exercise. Wearing such clothing for extended periods is dangerous and can lead to heat exhaustion, caused by the inhibition of sweat evaporation, and/or dehydration exhaustion, caused by lost fluids not being replaced. If continued, these two conditions will lead to heat stroke, a medical emergency.

MYTH:

It's not good to build muscle because it will change to fat when you stop exercising.

FACT:

Muscles can become flaccid but cannot metamorphose into fat.

Muscles do not turn to fat. They can atrophy and shrink, and their place can be taken by fat. If you stop exercising, your arm or waist could end up with essentially the same girth, but the composition would be different. Surprisingly, your scale might show that you weigh less, simply because fat weighs less than muscle.

Exercise and Women

MYTH:

Women cannot be as fit as men.

FACT:

Research on males and females with similar activity patterns shows that there is little difference in their strength, endurance and body composition ratings (J. P. Wilmore, "Exploding the Myth of Female Inferiority," The Physician and Sports Medicine).

The fact that national surveys find women to have slightly lower fitness levels than men in all the major components except flexibility can be attributed to cultural patterns which overprotect women and discourage them from exercising. Thus the difference in fitness between men and women is due to differences in physical activity habits, not biological factors.

MYTH:
Women require special guidelines to exercise safely.
FACT:
Women are no more susceptible to injury than men.

Studies are needed to address the question of the particular effects of exercise on women. However, at this point as far as we know, the same principles of training apply to men and women. Prevalence of injuries is determined by the strength of the muscles and ligaments involved. Cases of prolapsed uterus in runners occur primarily in women who have weak muscular and connective tissue after childbirth. This situation is usually detected in post-partum exams. Thus this injury is like others; it occurs if there is an existing weakness which cannot handle the stress placed on it. Further, women who exercise strenuously may need to be sensitive to extra nutritional needs, especially calcium and iron.

MYTH:
Weightlifting makes women ugly because of its masculinizing effects.
FACT:
Women do not bulk up to the same degree that men because they do not have the testosterone level that allows a muscle to grow excessively.

Moderate, gradual repetitions of lighter weights is a better lifting program than minimal, fast repetitions of heavier weights if you do not want to bulk up.

Exercise and Food

MYTH:

Carbohydrate loading guarantees a competitive advantage in an endurance event.

FACT:

It is good to derive 50 - 60% of your calories from carbohydrates all the time. The dietary practice known as carbohydrate loading, however, is not advisable for all types of exercise.

"Carbohydrate loading" involves a regimen of first creating carbohydrate deprivation by eliminating carbohydrates from your diet for a few days while engaging in intense workouts, and then loading up on carbohydrates in the days preceding the endurance event. The goal is to increase the body store of glycogen, providing enhanced energy for endurance events like marathons.

Research now indicates that this regimen can lead to significant health problems. The current recommendation for carbohydrate loading is to maintain intake of carbohydrates at 50 - 60% of total calories while engaged in endurance training, and then three days before an endurance event increase carbohydrate intake to 70% of total calories and reduce exercise. This has been shown to increase energy stores up to three times their normal levels.

Carbohydrate loading is not for everyone. It should be tested carefully during training and certainly should not be tried for the first time just before an athletic event. Research continues on this controversial topic.

MYTH:

Eating protein builds muscles.

FACT:

Use of muscles – not intake of excessive protein – is what builds muscles.

Dietary protein is in no way directly transformed into human muscle. Protein is necessary for the production of new cells in the body, but Americans on average get more than twice what they need for this purpose.

MYTH:

Exercise significantly increases vitamin and mineral needs.

FACT:

Exercise demands more calories. However, the vitamin and mineral requirements of a regular exerciser are not significantly different from a sedentary person's.

If you eat a well-balanced diet, including a variety of foods, the amount of vitamins you take in will be sufficient. Also, it has never been shown that a vitamin surplus will improve performance.

MYTH:

Restricting fluid intake is a recommended practice during training.

FACT:

Water is essential during any physical activity and should never be restricted.

Fluid should be consumed before, during, and after exercise, especially after prolonged activity in warm weather. Your body needs water to conduct the physical processes that occur during exercise. Waste products will be disposed of more efficiently with plenty of water.

MYTH:

You need salt tablets to replace sodium lost in sweat.

FACT:

Salt tablets are not recommended because an excessive salt intake puts extra burden on the kidneys.

There is seldom any need to replace sodium. On the average, Americans get more than 20 times as much as they need. If sodium is needed, it is best replaced by foods prepared for the next meal.

MYTH:

Commercial "thirst quencher" products replace vital minerals lost through heavy sweating.

FACT:

You can't beat water! Popular thirst quenchers formulated especially for athletes may contain large amounts of sodium, sugar, and other additives. They are generally not recommended.
Water is the best thirst quencher.

MYTH:

Eating foods high in sugar before exercising provides quick energy.

TRUTH:

How quick is "quick"? In this case it takes about 20 - 30 minutes before the energy from sugar becomes available to your muscles. Once it is accessed, sugar is burned up in minutes.

Large amounts of sugar before exercise can result in dehydration, stomach discomfort, and ironically, low blood sugar. The human body was not designed to cope with a sudden "hit" of sugar. It sends out a sudden rush of insulin to clear the sugar from the blood, and in fact, may send more insulin than necessary. Result: the sugar clears, and you are left with a high level of insulin that continues to lower your blood sugar, leaving you feeling less energetic than before. Complex carboydrates (rice, apples, whole grains), rather than simple carbohydrates (cookies, candy, honey), provide a long-lasting source of energy.

Exercise and the Later Years

MYTH:

The older you are, the less exercise you need.

FACT:

Middle-aged and older people benefit from regular exercise just as young people do.

With age we tend to become less physically active in our daily routine, and therefore need to make up for this with exercise. Age need not be a limitation. What is important, no matter what your age, is tailoring the exercise program to your own fitness level: for example, take an hour's walk instead of an hour's run.

MYTH:

Fitness naturally declines with age.

FACT:

Fitness declines with a decrease in activity. If you don't use it, you lose it!

MYTH:

Exercise is for the young.

FACT:

Exercise is for everyone!

Anyone can become more fit. And the less fit you are to start with, the more you will notice the physical and psychological benefits associated with an active lifestyle. Whatever your age, you can find an exercise routine that will improve the quality of your life!

If you are honest, you know that your stamina or endurance is not as good as it used to be when a last-minute dash through an airport causes you significant discomfort.

Exercise

How important is it to have some form of fitness evaluation before you start an exercise program? The answer depends upon a number of factors such as your age, current fitness level, general health, and what type of physical activity you plan to perform. If you are 60 years old, sedentary, overweight, have a history of heart disease, and have now decided to get back into shape for a Himalayan trek, your medical and physical evaluation needs are very different than those of a younger, active person of normal weight and no history of heart disease who plans to make the same trip.

The American College of Sports Medicine, the National Heart, Lung and Blood Institutes, The American Heart Association, and the Y.M.C.A have all made recommendations on the topic of pre-exercise medical and physical evaluations. A summary of their recommendations would suggest that young, active individuals who are at low risk for heart disease with no symptoms do not need to see a physician before starting an exercise program. However, older sedentary individuals without symptoms of heart disease may wish to consult with a physician, and individuals of any age with symptoms of heart disease are strongly encouraged to schedule medical and physical examinations before initiating an exercise program.

> **Tony Evans**, *Ph.D.,*
> *is research associate in the SCRDP and the Division of Cardiology, Stanford University School of Medicine, and project director of a National Institutes of Health funded Physical Activity Measurement Study.*

A practical self-test that was developed and used in Canada to help people determine if they needed a pre-exercise medical consultation is called the Physical Activity Readiness Questionaire (PAR-Q). This is another useful screening device for your use.

Physical Activity Readiness Questionnaire (PAR-Q)

For most people, physical activity should not pose any problem or hazard. PAR-Q has been designed to identify the small number of adults for whom physical activity might be inappropriate or those who should have medical advice concerning the type of activity most suitable for them. If you answer "yes" to any of the questions below, consult with your doctor before starting exercise.

1. Has your doctor ever said you have heart trouble?
   Yes   No

2. Do you frequently have pains in your heart and chest?
   Yes   No

3. Do you often feel faint or have spells of severe dizziness?
   Yes   No

4. Has a doctor ever told you that you have a bone or joint problem such as arthritis that has been aggravated by exercise, or might be made worse with exercise?
   Yes   No

5. Has a doctor ever said your blood pressure was too high?
   Yes   No

6. Is there a good physical reason not mentioned here why you should not follow an activity program if you want to?
   Yes   No

7. Are you over age 69 and not accustomed to vigorous exercise?
   Yes   No

Source: *British Columbia Medical Journal*, 17: 375-378, 1975.

For normal, healthy individuals, perhaps our own intuition is a sufficient evaluation of fitness. If you are honest, you know that your stamina or endurance is not as good as it used to be when a last-minute dash through an airport causes you significant discomfort. An increase in your clothes size, when you're well beyond adolescent growth spurts, is a reasonable clue that your girth and weight are expanding.

Of course, while some people's intuition is good, it doesn't give them the quantitative information that can motivate them to start an exercise program. The rest of this chapter offers some techniques for basic health and fitness self-evaluations that can provide some of this quantitative information. For each test, an explanation is provided, as well as some norms which you can use to compare yourself to others of the same age and sex. A fitness log is also included to help you chart your fitness scores over a period of time. This is a fun, motivational method to help you keep track of your fitness status as you follow your exercise program.

Testing Your Risk of Chronic Disease

Here's a useful test to get you going. It's a test that looks at a number of health behaviors associated with risk for heart attack and stroke.

Simplified Self-Scoring Test of Chronic Disease Risk					
Risk Habit or Factor			Increasing Risk		
I. Smoking Cigarettes	None	Up to 9 per day	10 to 24 per day	25 to 34 per day	35 or more per day
Score	0	1	2	3	4
II. Body Weight	Ideal weight	Up to 9 lbs. excess	10 to 19 lbs excess	20 to 29 lbs. excess	30 lbs or more excess
Score	0	1	2	3	4
III. Salt Intake or Blood Pressure Upper Reading (if known)	1/5 average hard to achieve; no added salt, no conven- ience foods Less than 110	1/3 average no use of salt at table, spare use of high-salt foods 110 to 129	U.S. average salt in cooking, some salt at table 130 to 139	Above average frequent salt at table 140 to 149	Far above average frequent use of salty foods 150 or over
Score	0	1	2	3	4

Simplified Self-Scoring Test of Chronic Disease Risk (cont'd)

Risk Habit or Factor	Increasing Risk				
IV. Saturated Fat and Cholesterol Intake *or* **Blood Cholesterol Level (if known)**	1/5 average almost total vegetarian; rare egg yolk, butterfat & lean meat	1/3 average 2 meatless days/week, no whole milk products, lean meat only	1/2 average meat (mostly lean), eggs, cheese 12 times/week, nonfat milk only	U.S. average meat, cheese, eggs, whole milk 24 times/week	Above average meat, cheese, eggs, whole milk over 24 times/week
	Less than 150	150 to 169	170 to 199	200 to 219	220 or over
Score	0	1	2	3	4
V. Self-Rating of Physical Activity *or* **Walking Rating**	Vigorous exercise 4 or more times/week 20 min. each Brisk walking 5 times/week 45 min. each	Vigorous exercise 3 times/week 20 min. each Brisk walking 3 times/week 30 min. each	Vigorous exercise 1 to 2 times/week Brisk walking 2 times/week 30 min. each or Normal walking 4 1/2 to 6 miles daily	U.S. average occasional exercise Normal walking 2 1/2 to 4 1/2 miles daily	Below average exercises rarely Normal walking less than 2 1/2 miles daily
Score	0	1	2	3	4
VI. Self-Rating of Stress and Tension	Rarely tense or anxious or Yoga, meditation, or equivalent 20 min. 2 times/day	Calmer than average Feel tense about 3 times/week	U.S. average Feel tense or anxious 2 to 3 times/day Frequent anger or hurried feelings	Quite tense Usually rushed Occasionally take tranquilizer	Extremely tense Take tranquilizer 5 times/week or more
Score	0	1	2	3	4

Enter your total score here _____.

Notes: 1) Subtract 1 point if dietary fiber intake is high (almost all cereals whole grain, almost no sugar, and considerable fruit and vegetable intake). 2) If you are a female taking estrogen or birth control pills, add 1 point if score is 12 or below, 2 points if risk score is 13 or above (especially if you smoke, are overweight, have high blood pressure or high blood cholesterol). 3) Add 1 point for each 10 points of blood pressure above 150 and 1 point for each 30 points of cholesterol above 220. 4) Subtract 1 point if high density cholesterol level (the protective cholesterol fraction that increases with exercise) is greater than 50.

INTERPRETATION

(Risks are given for cardiovascular disease. They apply, but with less precision, for adult-onset diabetes and diet-related cancers of the breast and colon. For smoking-related cancer of the lungs, the predominant risk is duration and amount of smoking.)

Zone	Score	(*Maximum points = 24*)
F	20-24	**The probability of having a premature heart attack or stroke is about four to five times the U.S. average. Action is urgent. Try to drop four points within a month and three more points within six months.**
E	16-19	**Incidence of heart attack or stroke is about twice the U.S. average. Action is urgent. Try to drop four points within six months and continue reduction.**
D	12-15	**The U.S. average is 13. This is an uncomfortable and readily avoidable zone. Careful planning can result in a five- to six-point reduction within a year.**
C	8-11	**The likelihood of having a heart attack or stroke is about one-half the U.S. average. This is a zone rather easily achieved by most people within a year if they arc now in Zone D or E. Careful planning can result in a four-to six-point reduction within a year.**
B	4-7	**Incidence of heart attack or stroke about one-quarter of the U.S. average This goal is achievable by many but often takes one to two years to reach.**
A	0-3	**Incidence of heart attack or stroke rates very low, averaging less than one-tenth the rate in the U.S. 35-65 age group. This goal requires diligent effort, considerable family support, and often takes three to four years to reach. Individuals in this range should be proud and gratified (and will often find themselves acting as models and teachers for the many who have not achieved this very low risk zone).**

Assessing Your Body Weight

Height and weight tables have frequently been used to help determine desirable weight for height. The drawback of this evaluation is that it does not account for variations in body composition (the ratio of fat to lean body weight). However height/weight tables are still useful to get an estimate of your weight for height so that you can determine your weight status in relation to obesity. The National Institute of Health's consensus panel on obesity recommends that two methods be used in the measurement of obesity. Following are self-tests for relative weight and body mass index.

The formula for assessing your relative weight is:

Relative Weight= Body weight/Midpoint value of weight range

Recommended Weights in Relation to Height		
HEIGHT	**WEIGHT**	
	MEN	**WOMEN**
58		92-121
59		95-124
60		98-127
61	105-134	101-130
62	108-137	104-134
63	111-141	107-138
64	114-145	110-142
65	117-149	114-146
66	121-154	118-150
67	125-159	122-154
68	129-163	126-159
69	133-167	130-164
70	137-172	134-169
71	141-177	
72	145-182	
73	149-187	
74	153-192	
75	157-197	

Now let's use this formula together with the 1959 Metropolitan weight tables as recommended by the American Heart Association and the example of a man who is 72" tall and weighs 190 pounds.

(This table was developed for the Fogarty International Conference on Obesity in 1973. The data is from the 1959 Metropolitan Life Insurance Company, adjusted to express height without shoes and weight without clothes.)

Source: Metropolitan Life Insurance Company Height and Weight Tables 1959

Relative Weight= 190/163.5 = 1.162

This person is 16.2% overweight. Twenty percent over-weight is considered obese.

The second method for measurement of obesity uses the Body Mass Index (BMI), which is simply body weight in kilograms/height in meters squared (1 kilogram=2.2 pounds and 1 inch= 2.54 centimeters).

For example, a 70-kilogram man standing 70 inches tall has a BMI of :

BMI= 70kg/1.778 m squared = 70/3.161 = 22.14

The Body Mass Index values for obesity which correspond with 20% above desirable weight are 27.2 for males and 26.9 for females repectively. Therefore, the male in our example with a BMI of 22.14 is well under the BMI of 27.2 that is associated with male obesity.

Determining Your Heart Rate

Resting heart rate is a simple and useful measure of physical fitness. Heredity frequently contributes to a low resting heart rate, and certain drugs can also reduce it. However, it is also well established that exercisc training of sufficient intensity also contributes to a lower resting heart rate. This is a simple evaluation that, when done correctly and charted over a period of time, provides useful information about the effectiveness of a fitness training program.

Before measuring your pulse, rest quietly for at least five minutes. Next, locate either your radial or carotid pulse (see diagram) and start counting your pulse beats for a full minute. Now compare your resting heart rate against the YMCA norms.

How to Monitor Your Exercise Pulse Rate

Or
Find your radial artery by pressing your fingers on the outside of your wrist just below your thumb.

2. Using a watch with a sweep hand or a digital read-out of seconds, count the number of times your heart beats in ten seconds.

1 .Locate your carotid artery with the tips of your third and fourth fingers. (The carotid artery is in the front strip of muscle than runs vertically down your neck.) Press fingers on one side only of the neck.

3. Compare the total number of beats for ten seconds with the appropriate target heart rate zone for your age and adjust your exercise intensity accordingly.

Source: Nash, J.D.: Maximize Your Body Potential. Bull Publishing Company, Palo Alto, California, 1986.

Norms for Resting Heart Rates for Males and Females
(Heart rates apply to all adult age groups)

	PERCENTILE	RHR MALES	RHR FEMALES
Exc	95	52	59
	85	59	63
	75	65	68
Avg	50	72	73
	30	78	80
	15	84	85
Poor	5	93	92

Source: Golding, L.A., Myers, C.R., and Sinning, W.W.: The Y's Way to Physical Fitness. National Board of the Y.M.C.A. Chicago, 1982.

Evaluating Your Blood Pressure

Resting blood pressure is another useful fitness measure that, when measured accurately, provides important information about the condition of the cardiovascular system, especially the stress under which the heart is having to pump blood around this closed circuit. Numerous inexpensive blood measuring devices are available that can be used at home. However, this measurement does require precision, and the most you can expect from the automated systems on the market or in pharmacies is a crude estimate of blood pressure. Everyone should know their blood pressure. It is a major risk factor together with cholesterol and smoking. If you don't know your blood pressure, get it checked by your physician or other trained professional. They can interpret your result for you. Here are norms for resting blood pressure provided by the Joint Committee on Detection, Evaluation, and Treatment of High Blood Pressure.

Assessing Your Cardiovascular Endurance

A measure of cardiovascular endurance is particularly important in any physical fitness evaluation because it indicates how efficiently we utilize oxygen in the cells of the body, especially the muscle cells. Higher levels of cardiovascular endurance indicate higher levels of fitness.

Norms for Resting Blood Pressure

(These readings are based on the average of two or more measurements taken on two or more occasions in the same individual 18 years and older.)

DIAST. BP	CLASS	SYSTOLIC BP	CLASS
<85	Normal	Less than 140	Normal
85-89	High normal	140-159	Borderline Systolic HTX
90-104	Mild HTX[1]	>160	Systolic HTX
105-114	Moderate HTX		
>115	Severe HTX		

HTX=hypertension

Source: *Report of the Joint Committee on Detection, Evaluation and Treatment of High Blood Pressure. 1984.*

Before describing a few valid methods for determining cardiovascular endurance that can be done at home, let's consider some basic cardiovascular training effects. Once you understand these, you can set up an even simpler, but still accurate, method to determine improvement in your cardiovascular system in response to an exercise training program.

As the heart gets stronger and becomes a more efficient pump, it requires fewer beats at rest and during any sub-maximal exercise effort. The ability of the heart to recover after exercise also improves. Now, with this information, let's make up our own test of cardiovascular endurance.

This test won't tell you how much oxygen you are using like the other tests included in this chapter, but it will let you know if your cardiovascular endurance is improving.

Simply walk or jog or walk/jog around a track, a block in your neighborhood or some other route that you can repeat in the future. (The distance must be the same each time you do the test). Immediately after your exercise, record the time it took you to complete the distance and measure your pulse rate for one full minute following your exercise. This is your *recovery heart rate*. Record this information in a log. After a couple of weeks of following your exercise training program, repeat this test. Of course, as you improve, two things will happen. Your times will decrease and so will your recovery heart rate.

Now let's consider simple tests you can do which will give you an estimate of your maximal oxygen uptake. To get an accurate measure of this requires a graded exercise test where oxygen consumption is measured directly.

Predicted maximal oxygen consumption based on performance of a 12-minute run

Distance (Miles)	Laps (1/4 Mile Track)	Predicted Maximal O_2 Uptake (ml/kg/min)
1.000	4	28.2
1.065	4 1/4	30.0
1.125	4 1/2	31.9
1.187	4 3/4	33.8
1.250	5	35.7
1.317	5 1/4	37.5
1.375	5 1/2	39.2
1.437	5 3/4	41.0
1.500	6	42.7
1.565	6 1/4	44.6
1.625	6 1/2	46.4
1.687	6 3/4	48.2
1.750	7	50.0
1.817	7 1/4	51.8
1.875	7 1/2	53.5
1.937	7 3/4	55.3
2.000	8	57.0

Source: Falls, H.B., Baylor, A.M., and Dishman, R.K.: Essentials of Fitness. Saunders, Holt, Rinehart and Winston. 1980.

The 12-Minute Run Test

This test was developed by Dr. Kenneth Cooper, based on

earlier work done by Dr. Bruno Balke. All you need to do is determine how far you can go by running and walking in a 12-minute period. A running track is an ideal location to conduct this test, but any place where you can get an accurate measure of distance is suitable. After completing the test and determining the distance you covered you can determine your predicted maximal oxygen uptake from the preceding table.

The One-and-a-Half-Mile Run

In this test it is important again to have a track or some other facility or route that is measured precisely. The object of this test is to cover the 1.5-mile run in the shortest time possible. This type of test requires a basic level of fitness to ensure that the test can be conducted safely. After completing the test, obtain an estimate of your maximum oxygen consumption from the accompanying table.

The Three-Minute Step Test

This test is not quite as convenient as the other cardiovascular endurance tests, but if you have access to some basic equipment, it's still one that is fairly easy to conduct. All you need is a 12" bench or step, a metronome that is set at 96 beats per minute (if you don't have a metronome, tape this beat from a friend who does), and a timer of any description that also has a second hand.

It's important first of all to practice stepping to the beat of the metronome. At 96 beats per minute and a four-count stepping rhythm (right foot up, left foot up, right foot down, left foot down), that results in 24 steps per minute. As soon as you are comfortable with the stepping

An Estimate of Maximal Oxygen Consumption Based on the Time Taken to Complete 1.5 Miles	
VO$_2$ MAX (ML/KG/MIN)	1.5 MILE RUN MIN:SEC
14.0	
17.5	
21.0	
24.5	
28.0	18:45
31.5	16:30
35.0	15:00
38.5	13:00
42.0	12:00
45.5	11:00
49.0	10:00
52.5	9:30
56.0	9:00
59.5	8:15
63.0	7:45
66.5	7:15
70.0	6:52
73.5	6:30
77.0	6:10

Source: Neiman, D.C.: The Sports Medicine Fitness Course. Bull Publishing Company, Palo Alto, CA 1986.

technique, you simply step up and down on the bench at a rate of 24 steps per minute for three minutes. After completing three minutes of exercise you sit down and immediately count your pulse rate for a full minute of recovery. This is your recovery heart rate, or your post-exercise one-minute heart rate. Compare your recovery heart rate to the following YMCA norms. If you are unable to complete the full three minutes of stepping, sit down immediately after you stop and count your pulse for a full minute of recovery. Record your one-minute post-exercise recovery heart rate and also how long you were able to do the test. You will not be able to compare your results to the norms provided but over time you will see your recovery heart rate reduce and your ability to complete the test improve.

Norms for Recovery Heart Rate (RHR) and Estimates of Maximal Oxygen Consumption (ml/kg/min) for Adult Men and Women.

	Percentile	Male		Female	
		RHR	ml/kg/min	RHR	ml/kg/min
Excellent	95	81-90	43-54	79-84	46-55
	85	99-102	38-49	90-97	38-45
	75	103-112	34-46	106-109	32-39
Average	50	120-121	30-36	118-119	27-34
	30	123-125	27-32	122-124	24-30
	15	127-130	24-28	129-134	20-26
Poor	5	136-138	20-24	137-145	18-20

(Recovery heart rate is taken while seated for one full minute after completing the step test.)

Source: Golding, L.A., Myers, C.R., and Sinning, W.W.: The Y's Way to Physical Fitness. National Board of the Y.M.C.A. Chicago, 1982.

All the cardiovascular endurance tests shown in this chapter provide you with predictions and estimations of maximal oxygen consumption in milliliters of oxygen per kilogram of your body weight per minute (ml/kg/min). The following table allows you to compare your estimate of maximal oxygen consumption with other people of similar age and sex.

Norms for Maximal Oxygen Consumption in Milliliters of Oxygen per Kilogram of Body Weight per Minute

WOMEN	LOW	FAIR	AVG	GOOD	HIGH	ATHL	OLYM
20-29	<28	29-34	35-43	44-48	49-53	54-59	60+
30-39	<27	28-33	34-41	42-47	48-52	53-58	59+
40-49	<25	26-31	32-40	41-45	46-50	51-56	57+
50-65	<21	22-28	29-36	37-41	42-45	46-49	50+
MEN							
20-29	<38	39-43	44-51	52-56	57-62	63-69	70+
30-39	<34	35-39	40-47	48-51	52-57	58-64	65+
40-49	<30	31-35	36-43	44-47	48-53	54-60	61+
50-59	<25	26-31	32-39	40-43	44-48	49-55	56+
60-69	<21	22-26	27-35	36-39	40-44	45-49	50+

Source: Neiman, D.C.: The Sports Medicine Fitness Course. Bull Publishing Company, Palo Alto, California, 1986.

Tests for Muscular Endurance and Strength

The first test evaluates strength and endurance of the abdominal muscles, an important muscle group especially for people trying to recover from chronic low back problems. This test is simply a bent-knee sit-up test. However, instead of holding your arms behind your head, just fold them across your chest. It's also appropriate to anchor your feet or have a friend hold them for you.

Canadian Norms for the Number of Sit-Ups Completed in 60 Seconds

MALES	Age	17-19	20-29	30-39	40-49	50-59	60-65
	Exc	>54	>51	>44	>38	>33	>33
	Good	44-53	40-50	34-43	29-37	25-32	23-32
	Min	34-43	30-39	25-33	20-28	16-24	13-22
	<Min	24-33	20-29	15-24	11-19	7-15	4-12
	Poor	<23	<19	<14	<10	<6	<3
FEMALES							
	Exc	>46	>41	>33	>28	>22	>23
	Good	35-45	31-40	24-32	20-27	14-21	15-22
	Min	24-34	21-30	15-23	12-19	6-13	7-14
	<Min	14-23	11-20	6-14	3-11	0-5	0-6
	Poor	<13	<10	<5	0-5		

Source: Fitness and Amateur Sport, Canada. Canadian Public Health Association Project. 1977.

A correct sit-up is recorded each time you sit up and touch your thighs with your crossed arms. Your final score is the number of correct sit-ups you have performed in 60 seconds. Now compare your performance to the norms.

The push-up test is another good evaluation of muscular strength and endurance, especially in the upper limbs.

This test simply requires you to complete as many push-ups as you can. The typical push-up is performed by men and a modified push-up from a bent knee position is done by women. Your score can then be compared to the following table.

Canadian Norms for the Completed Number of Pushups in 60 Seconds.							
MALES	Age	17-19	20-29	30-39	40-49	50-59	60-65
	Exc	>51	>43	>37	>31	>28	>27
	Good	35-50	30-42	25-36	21-30	18-27	17-26
	Min	19-34	17-29	13-24	11-20	9-17	6-16
	<Min	4-18	4-16	2-12	1-10	0-8	0-5
	Poor	<3	<3	<1	0		
FEMALES	Exc	>32	>33	>34	>28	>23	>21
MODIFIED	Good	21-31	23-32	22-33	18-27	15-22	13-20
PUSH-UPS	Min	11-20	12-22	10-21	8-17	7-14	5-12
	<Min	0-10	1-11	0-9	0-7	0-6	0-4
	Poor		0				

Source: Fitness and Amateur Sport, Canada. Canadian Public Health Association Project. 1977.

Evaluating Flexibility

A basic flexibility test that evaluates flexibility in the trunk can be done by placing a yardstick on the ground which is taped across at right angles to the 15" mark. Now sit with the yardstick between your legs and place your feet about 10 - 12" apart at right angles to the 15" mark. You should not wear shoes. Now slowly reach forward with both hands as far as possible on the yardstick. Your furthest reach on the yardstick should be done smoothly and with both hands together. The score recorded is the most distant point reached on the yard-stick in inches. The best score of three attempts is recorded. It is important to keep your knees straight during this test, and sometimes a spouse, family member, or friend can help ensure that your knees are maintained in the correct position. Once again, compare your score to the following table.

Each one of your fitness scores can be recorded in the following log and updated in subsequent logs to provide you with a simple, quantitative record of your fitness status. This type of record keeping has been shown to be very useful in motivating people to start a personal fitness program and maintain it. If you are interested in trying to start a personal fitness program but have been frustrated by previous futile attempts, give this a try.

Women: <35 years, 35-45 years, >45 years				
Percentage Ranking	Rating	Trunk Flexion Ins.	Trunk Flexion Ins.	Trunk Flexion Ins.
95	Excellent	23	23	22
85	Good	21	21	19
75	Above Av.	20	19	18
50	Average	18	17	15
30	Below Av.	15	14	14
15	Fair	14	12	11
5	Poor	11	10	9

Men: <35 years, 35-45 years, >45 years				
Percentage Ranking	Rating	Trunk Flexion Ins.	Trunk Flexion Ins.	Trunk Flexion Ins.
95	Excellent	21	22	20
85	Good	19	19	17
75	Above Av.	17	16	15
50	Average	15	14	13
30	Below Av.	12	12	11
15	Fair	9	10	8
5	Poor	7	5	5

Source: Golding, L.A., Myers, C.R., and Sinning, W.W.: The Y's Way to Physical Fitness. National Board of the Y.M.C.A. Chicago, 1982.

WEEKLY ACTIVITY LOG

DAY	AEROBICS TYPE/DURATION		PUSH UPS NUMBER	SIT UPS NUMBER	FLEXIBILITY CHECK
1					
2					
3					
4					
5					
6					
7					

MONTHLY FITNESS LOG

Fitness measure	Jan	Feb	Mar	Apr	May	Jun	July	Aug	Sept	Oct	Nov	Dec
Relative Weight												
Body Mass Index												
Resting Heart Rate												
Resting Blood Pressure												
12-Minute Run												
1.5-Mile Run												
Step Test VO$_2$ Max												
Sit-ups												
Push-ups												
Flexibility												

*T*he challenge is not starting a program so much as maintaining one for
the rest of your life.

Starting

T he way to fitness is through exercise. In this chapter, we will outline the steps you can take to create your personal exercise program and maintain it in your daily life. In the process, we will help you do the following:

1. Get Moving

• Make a firm commitment to exercise, whether you take up new activities or find a more active way to do the things you do now.

2. Build Up Slowly

• Make sure that it is medically safe to start.
• Take time to get fit, so you don't feel un-comfortable during or after the activity.
• Warm up and cool down, to help avoid injury.
• Increase the amount of activity by no more than 10% each week.

> **Barbara Frey-Hewitt**, M.S., is exercise physiologist, SCRDP, co-author of articles published by the American Dietetic Association and Medicine and Science in Sports and Exercise, and is the exercise leader in the Stanford Health & Exercise Video.

3. Do It Regularly

• Get into the habit of regular exercise, at least 20 minutes, three times a week.
• If you find you have a list of excuses for not exercising regularly (such as "too tired" or "no time") write them down and then refer to the other chapters in this book for help. You will probably find your most cherished excuses exploded there.

•Consider joining a class, or arrange to exercise with a friend. This will make it harder for you to change your mind at the last minute.

•Schedule your exercise in advance on your calendar.

4. Maintain the Program

•You're only fit so long as you exercise. You will need to find ways to keep up the regular exercise habit.

•Set realistic goals that you can achieve.

•Promise yourself a reward after three months (or decide to enter a sporting event, and set that as your goal).

•Tell everyone you know that you have begun an exercise program. They will help hold you to it.

Are You Ready to Begin?

Will you need a medical examination before you start? Probably not. For most people, starting an exercise program will pose no hazard. Almost everybody can safely exercise at some level of intensity, following the guidelines outlined later in this chapter. However, three categories of people might benefit from a medical check up:

•Those who have a history of heart disease, high blood pressure, lung disease, or disease of the bones or joint which could be made worse by excessive exercise.

•Those over 35 who have been previously sedentary and intend to plunge immediately into exercise that is more vigorous than brisk walking.

•Those who would be interested in finding out their current level of fitness, out of curiosity, and use it as a benchmark against which to measure future progress.

Medical Evaluations

At its simplest level, a medical evaluation might consist of a conversation with your regular physician. At its most complex, an evaluation might be carried out by an exercise specialist and would include evaluations of body composition, flexibility, and blood lipids. It would also include a treadmill or bicycle test to evaluate cardiovascular function and functional capacity (the amount of oxygen you can process at peak demand).

Although medical evaluations certainly have their place, they also have their drawbacks. A medical exam is expensive and does not guarantee that you will be immune to heart attacks during exercise.

In general, any person under 65 with no overt heart disease, high blood pressure, or orthopedic condition can start a gradual program of walking, bicycling, or swimming without undue risk.

Building Strength

Most of the time you spend in physical activity will probably be devoted to exercise that builds cardiovascular endurance. It is also important to spend time building strength. Unless strength is conscientiously maintained, it will decline with an inactive life-style, making routine tasks (and exercise itself) harder to perform. Strength-building exercises may be needed to keep your body's development in balance. For example, if your main exercise is walking or jogging, which uses your leg and back muscles, it is advisable to develop stomach and arm muscles with the following sit-ups and push-ups:

Sit-ups and push-ups prescription

Beginners should start with 3 sets of 5 sit-ups or push-ups with a rest between sets and gradually work up to 3 sets of 10 repetitions. Those in good shape can start with sets of 10. Do these at least 3 times a week. As your muscular endurance improves adjust your repetitions accordingly.

As an alternative, take an aerobic or calisthenics class which provides strengthening exercises for arms, legs, back, and stomach. Or use weight-training equipment. Start at a health club or gym where you can get instruction on safe and effective technique, or purchase equipment from a retailer who will explain its use. In general:

- For developing muscle endurance, use lighter weights and do many repetitions.
- For developing muscle power, use more resistance and fewer repetitions.
- If an exercise hurts, stop!
- Given the choice, use a weight-training machine rather than free weights, such as barbells. Machines ensure that you hold a good body position.

Flexibility

Flexibility is important for a number of reasons:

- to prevent injury while exercising
- to allow for flowing movement in daily living
- to help prevent low back problems.

Exercises that maintain flexibility are included in the section on "warming up," starting on page 71. Remember, it is important to stretch *moderately*, hold the stretch for 20 - 30 seconds, and *don't bounce*. Although some stretching exercises are specific to the sport you perform, there are many that are useful in promoting overall flexibility for everyone, no matter what endurance-building activity you choose.

Cardiovascular Endurance

To achieve cardiovascular fitness, exercise must produce a sustained elevation in metabolic, cardiovascular, and respiratory functions. In the process, the cardiovascular system must supply oxygen steadily to the exercising muscle for fuel: hence the term "aerobic," meaning "with oxygen." Any activity that can be maintained continuously, is rhythmical, and uses large muscle groups is considered an aerobic exercise. The most common aerobic activities include:

Brisk walking	Jogging	Skating
Cycling (10 mph)	Swimming	Skiing
Tennis (singles)	Rowing	Aerobic dance

Activities like tennis (doubles) or golf (if you ride in a cart) are not sufficiently vigorous to enhance cardiovascular endurance, while games like softball are not sufficiently continuous. However, they are excellent recreational activities.

The Three Phases of Exercise

Exercise sessions should consist of:

1. A ten-minute warm-up period, including general movements to warm up the cardiovascular system and stretching exercises to prepare the joints being used.
2. A 20- to 60- minute "stimulus" period, the aerobic portion for improving your cardiovascular endurance.
3. A five- to ten-minute cool-down period, including further stretching and strengthening exercises.

Warm-Up and Cool-Down

For some, these may seem the most boring parts of any exercise program. However, both phases are important to:

• prevent injury
• balance muscle development
• prepare the cardiovascular system for strenuous activity or calm it down afterwards.

In general, the warm-up should follow this pattern:
1. Slow, large movements such as arm circling, arm swinging, and slow walking.

2. Stretches, including those which are exercise-specific and stretches for flexibility of the neck, shoulders, trunk, hip, hamstring, calves, and Achilles tendon. The general rules for stretches are:

- Do not bounce or jerk.
- Hold the stretch at a degree of mild tension (before the muscle begins to shake) for approximately 20 - 30 seconds.
- Stretch the area two to three times.

During cooldown, walk around for a few minutes until your breathing rate and heart rate have gone down; then repeat the same stretches you did in the warm-up.

The "Stimulus" Period

During the main part of your exercise session, there are three important issues:

- whether you are enjoying yourself
- whether you are doing the exercise safely, without risk of damage to your joints, muscles, or heart
- whether you are exercising intensely enough.

The first question is plainly important: If you are miserable, you'll probably quit. It's obviously worthwhile to look for an exercise you like, to prevent boredom by mixing different types of exercise, and to arrange for pleasant company while you work out.

The second and third issues will depend on the intensity with which you exercise.

Intensity

There is a required intensity that is needed to condition the cardiovascular system, producing the overload that leads to physical fitness. For cardiovascular endurance, this level of intensity can be determined in two ways: first, by the amount of oxygen you are capable of using during exhaustive work (known as your VO_2max) and second, by the speed of your heart. Obtaining your VO_2max requires a graded exercise test measuring your inhaled and expired air (see p. 23). Luckily, the VO_2max corresponds closely to your maximal attainable heart rate, which is much simpler to calculate, since it depends largely on your age. Your maximal heart rate will be 220, minus your age. During exercise, your heart should reach a "target heart rate" of between 60% and 85% of the maximum – the low end for beginners, the high end for those who are already fit.

To find your exercising heart rate, wait until you are well warmed-up, and have been exercising for at least five minutes. Count your pulse either at your wrist or (gently!) at the artery about one inch to the side of your windpipe. Count for 6 seconds and multiply by 10 (or count for 10 seconds and multiply by 6). If your pulse is below the "target heart rate" in the chart, then you need to speed up. If your heart rate goes above the range (or for beginners, above 70%) then the work is too vigorous and you need to slow down. Here are

	Target Heart Rate Zone		
Age	Estimated Maximum Heart Rate	Beats Per Minute 60% - 85%	Beats Per 10 Seconds of Maximum
20	200	120-170	20-28
25	195	117-166	20-28
30	190	114-162	19-27
35	185	111-157	19-26
40	180	108-153	18-26
45	175	105-149	18-25
50	170	102-145	17-24
55	165	99-140	17-23
60	160	96-136	16-23
65	155	93-132	16-22
70	150	90-128	15-21
75	145	87-123	15-21
80	140	84-119	14-20

Adapted from Maximize Your Body Potential, Joyce D. Nash, Ph.D. Bull Publishing Company. Palo Alto, 1986. Page 82

some other tips to help you achieve the right level of intensity:
• Use the "talk test." If you cannot talk comfortably while exercising, then you are working too hard (and if you can talk with great ease, you need to work harder).
• Use your "rating of perceived exertion," or "RPE," as it was named by its inventor, Dr. G. Borg. He suggested a scale of 6 - 20 to describe how hard people feel they are exerting themselves (with 6 as very light and 20, very, very hard). On that scale, an RPE of 12 corresponds to a heart rate of 120 beats a minute and moderately hard exertion and an RPE of 17 to a heart rate of 170 and very hard exertion – and so on.
• In brief, listen to your body and let your heart rate and feeling of exertion be your inner coach. After the more strenuous part of the exercise, move around slowly for five minutes, or until your pulse is well below the target zone. Then perform another set of stretching exercises, while your muscles are warm and pliable.

Duration and Frequency of Exercise

In addition to a ten-minute warm-up period (and a five-to ten-minute cool-down) the period of exercise should last at least 20 minutes. As you become fitter, you will benefit by increasing this "stimulus" period to 40 or even 60 minutes. The recommended frequency is every other day. On your "off" days, continue the conditioning process by increasing your routine activity (walking, gardening, cleaning cars or houses, etc.)

Caloric Expenditure

If you like, you may now forget the previous advice on duration and frequency of exercise. Use instead a system that involves keeping track of caloric expenditure. This may be of particular interest to those losing weight, but can give everyone a useful way to monitor the amount of exercise they are getting.

Conveniently, caloric expenditure can be tied to heart rate. A minute of continuous exercise at about 60% of maximum will use up about eight calories a minute. At 80%, you will burn ten calories a minute.

As you can see from the chart, the recommended caloric expenditure for beginners (those who have been sedentary for a while) is about 1,000 calories a week. This is derived from three 20-minute periods of activity in the target heart rate zone; one hour of stretches and strength exercises; and one hour of additional routine activity (such as walking or yard work). For those who have reached a

Recommended amounts of physical activity done per week for apparently healthy adults

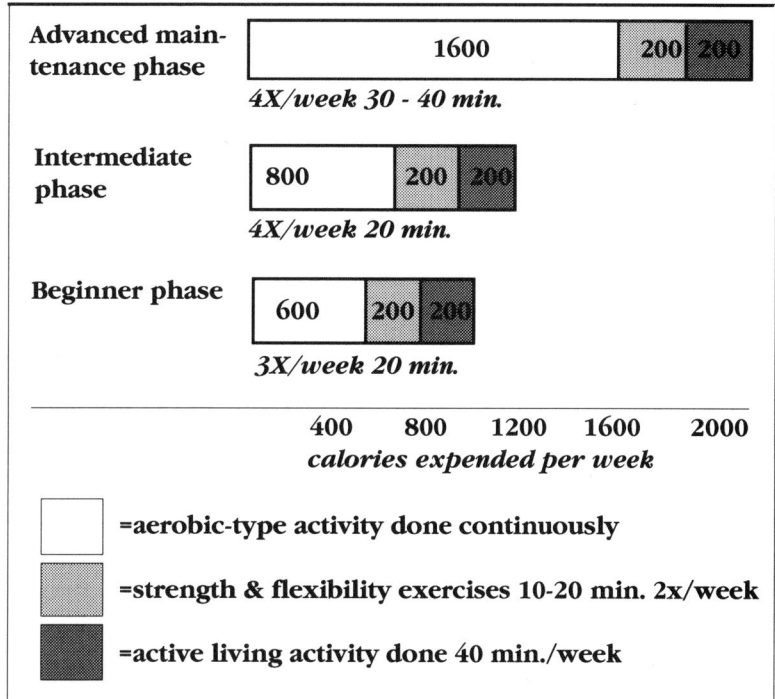

Advanced maintenance phase	1600		200	200

4X/week 30 - 40 min.

Intermediate phase	800		200	200

4X/week 20 min.

Beginner phase	600	200	200

3X/week 20 min.

400   800   1200   1600   2000
calories expended per week

☐ =aerobic-type activity done continuously

▨ =strength & flexibility exercises 10-20 min. 2x/week

▨ =active living activity done 40 min./week

high level of fitness, and who exercise for longer periods of time, the number of calories rises to about 2,000 a week. Charts which tell you how many calories are used up by a specific type of exercise may be misleading, since it depends on the weight of the exerciser: Someone of 225 pounds will use up twice as many calories as someone weighing 112. However, the number of calories per minute used up at (say) 70% of maximal capacity is about the same for everyone, no matter what the weight or degree of fitness. The fit person just has to work harder to get to that maximal capacity.

Selection of Exercise

In selecting a type of exercise, we suggest that you mix two or more types: Your physical development will be better balanced, and there will be less risk of boredom. Here are some advantages and disadvantages of different types, with some practical suggestions on ways to make the most of each activity.

Walking Briskly (Striding)

Walking briskly is good exercise at any age, and by far the best all-around exercise for those who have been out of shape for a while, who are overweight, or who are getting older. Walking regularly will help keep you mobile, and walking is an excellent way to relieve stress. It is also the best way to involve all family members in an activity.

Brisk walking that brings your heart to its target zone will build endurance, but will do little for flexibility, strength and agility. For all-around fitness, it is wise to take some other form of exercise as well.

• "Power" walking or striding (with arm movements as vigorous as those used in jogging) will raise the heart rate more effectively than regular walking.

• Walk without carrying anything, so you can swing your arms.

• Wear strong, comfortable shoes that offer the flexibility to roll through your stride, as your foot lands on the outer heel then rolls to push off with the toe. Also, wear thick socks.

Jogging and Running

Like walking, this is a cheap, convenient, and quick way to get fit. It's very good for developing endurance, but not so good for flexibility and upper body or stomach strength. There is a risk of overuse injuries to the feet, ankles, knees, and hips. However, if you progress slowly and run on softer surfaces with good shoes, you should not have serious difficulties (though if you are over-weight or have any orthopedic problems such as arthritis, swim-ming, or cycling are better choices.)

• Buying good shoes is the only expense in running; look for a pair that holds your heel securely and has good shock absorp-tion.

Swimming

If there is an ideal exercise, it is swimming. It strengthens the body, builds endurance and promotes flexibility and agility. It's a great way to get fit, if you have easy access to a pool, and you know how to swim! Swimming is especially good for overweight or disabled people.

• If you need to improve your technique, ask about lessons at your local pool.

Cycling

Cycling is great for developing endurance and leg strength, but will not promote flexibility. Regular bicycling around town is more entertaining than the stationary type, though it can be hard to keep the pedaling intensity high enough to get your heart working. With stationary cycling, this is not a problem; boredom, however, is.

• Watch TV or read while using a stationary bicycle.
• If you use a regular bicycle, include some uphill pedaling to give your heart a sufficient workout.
• Rent a stationary bike to try out before you invest in one. (There's a high ratio of stored to active bikes!)

Keeping It Up

The challenge is not starting a program so much as maintaining one for the rest of your life; and the hardest part of exercise may be keeping it up after the first feelings of virtue have worn off. An exercise prescription should include strategies for dealing with these problems, even before they have come up. Obviously, it is important not to set up goals you are unlikely to reach, either in terms of time or effort. And while it is very useful to plan ahead, it is also important not to set up a schedule so rigid that you can't meet its demands and feel guilty as a result. Planning one week's activity at a time is helpful, especially if you arrange to exercise with someone else (thus making it hard to change your mind at the last minute).

ONE EXAMPLE OF AN OUTLINE FOR AN EXERCISE PROGRAM

1. WARM-UP
   a. Purpose—To slowly elevate the pulse to an aerobic level
   b. What to do—Engage in 2-5 minutes of walking, slow jogging, light   calisthenics (arm circles, trunk circling, jumping jacks)

2. CARDIOVASCULAR—AEROBIC SESSION
   a. Purpose—To elevate the heart rate between 60-85% of maximum, depending on fitness level, for 10-60 minutes (at least 3 days/week)
   b. Guidelines for Aerobic Exercise Prescription

Factor (Think FIT)	Low Fitness	Average Fitness	High Fitness
F Frequency (days/week)	3	3-4	5+
I Intensity (% maximum heart rate range)	60-70	65-75	70-85
T Time (continuous minutes/ workout)	10-20	15-45	30-60
Mode Examples—(plus other continuous, rhythmical activities like swimming, cycling, skating, skiing, etc.)	Brisk Walking	Walk/Jog	Running

Your RHR _____   Max. HR _____   Your training HR _____   10 Sec. pulse count _____
(as determined by treadmill testing, or 220 minus age)   (Karvonen for- mula)*

Days/time you plan to exercise
(allow 1 hour for warm up, exercise, cool down, and calisthenics)

Sun.	Mon.	Tues.	Wed.	Thurs.	Fri.	Sat.
____am/pm	____am/pm	____am/pm	____am/pm	____am/pm	____am/pm	____am/pm

3. COOL-DOWN
   a. Purpose—to slowly decrease pulse rate, safely, by keeping on feet, legs moving

4.   FLEXIBILITY
   a. Purpose—To stretch major muscle groups, especially those involved in the exercise

b.   **What to do – Use static stretch positions for 5-10 minutes**

5.   **CONDITIONING CALISTHENICS**
   a.   **Purpose – To build muscular endurance and strength, especially in the muscles not developed through the aerobic activity**
   b.   **What to do – Bent knee sit-ups, push-ups, weight lifting, chin-ups, circuit training, etc.**

The training heart rates are based on a participant's maximum heart rates recorded during a medically supervised exercise treadmill test. If you don't have this information, you can obtain an estimate of your maximum heart rate by subtracting your age from 220.

Karvonen Formula for determining training heart rate is calculated as follows:

   (220 - age) - Resting Heart Rate x 70 to 85% + resting heart rate.

Example of a 45 year old with resting heart rate of 75, training at 70% intensity:

   (220 - 45) - 75 x 70% + 75 = Training Heart Rate of 145 beats per minute, or 24 beats in 10 seconds.

Adapted from Nieman, D.C., The Sports Medicine Fitness Course. Bull Publishing Company, Palo Alto, California.

EXAMPLES OF AEROBIC EXERCISE PROGRAMS FOR PARTICIPANTS IN A STANFORD HOME-BASED, SELF-MONITORED EXERCISE PROGRAM.

HIGHER INTENSITY INDIVIDUAL CONDITION

Name: _____ **Goode Hart** _____   Date: _____ **10/3/87** _____

During your recent treadmill exercise test you attained a maximal heart rate of __180__ bpm and oxygen uptake of __30__ ml/kg/min. Based on this test, your training heart rate range is __131__ to __155__ bpm or __22__ to __26__ in 10 seconds. Please follow this exercise plan.

Week	Sessions/week	Training Heart Rate (10 secs)	Minutes/session
1-2	3	60% MHR = __18__	20
3-4	3	65% MHR = __20__	25
5-6	3	73% MHR = __22__	30
7-8	3	73% MHR + 12 = __22__ to __24__	35
9+	3	73% MHR + 24 = __22__ to __26__	40

Do not progress to the next level if you are having problems (leg pains, long-lasting fatigue).

LOWER INTENSITY INDIVIDUAL CONDITION

Name: _____ **Goode Hart** _____   Date: _____ **10/3/87** _____

During your recent treadmill exercise test you attained a maximal heart rate of __180__ bpm and oxygen uptake of __30__ ml/kg/min. Based on this test, your training heart rate range is __108__ to __132__ bpm or __18__ to __22__ in 10 seconds. Please follow this exercise plan.

Week	Sessions/Week	Heart Rate (10 seconds)	Minutes/Session
1	Every other day	60% x MHR = __18__	20
2	Every other day	60% x MHR = __18__	25
3	5	60% x MHR + 12 = __18__ to __20__	30
4	5	60% x MHR + 24 = __18__ to __22__	30

Do not progress to the next level if you are having problems (leg pain, long-lasting fatigue).

DAILY EXERCISE TRAINING LOG

NAME: _____ GOODE HART
CONDITIONING HEART RATE __131__ to __155__ beats/min or __22__ to __26__ beats/10 seconds

INSTRUCTIONS: For each day in which you carry out any physical activity, please record each of the following. (For days you carry out no physical activity, record an "X" in the activity column.)

1. *Type* of conditioning activity as follows:
   W = Walk   W/J = Walk/Jog   C = Cycle
2. *Heart rate* at end of exercise session. Record # of beats/10 seconds.
3. *Duration* of this activity within the training range.
4. *Rate of perceived exertion* recorded during this activity. (Peak RPE is a subjective rating of the highest level of exertion during exercise).

LEVEL OF EXERTION

6	7	9	11	13	15	17	19	20
ex-tremely light	very, very light	very light	fairly light	somewhat hard	hard	very hard	very, very hard	ex-tremely hard

5. *Overall level of enjoyment* for each exercise session.

LEVEL OF ENJOYMENT

1	2	3	4	5	6	7	8	9	10
not at all enjoyable				moderately enjoyable				very enjoyable	

6. *Level of convenience* for each exercise session.

LEVEL OF CONVENIENCE

1	2	3	4	5	6	7	8	9	10
not at all convenient			moderately convenient				very convenient		

7. *Comments*: Change in symptoms, problems, special circumstances, any additional physical activity.

Sample Exercise Log

DAY	DATE	ACTIVITY	HR	DURATION	PEAK RPE	ENJOYMENT	CONVENIENCE	COMMENTS
1	10/5	W	23	25	13	8	8	Walking exercise fun and relaxing. No problems.
2	10/6	XX						No exercise today.
3	10/7	W	23	25	13	8	8	Another good walking session.

People come up with an array of excuses that are quite breathtaking in their ingenuity and diversity.

Excuses

When people have been exercising regularly for a few months, they tend to become hooked: they wouldn't quit if you paid them to. But getting started, and staying with exercise for the first critical months, may not be easy. Indeed, people can come up with an array of excuses that are quite breathtaking in their ingenuity and diversity. In this chapter, we will examine some of the more common (and uncommon) excuses that people produce that may develop into permanent barriers unless they are confronted and systematically dismantled.

> *June A. Flora*, *Ph.D., and* *Prudence Breitrose*, *M.A. Dr. Flora is associate director, SCRDP, and assistant professor of communications, Stanford University. Ms. Breitrose is health communications specialist, Stanford Health Promotion Resource Center, and was formerly with BBC television, London.*

The Diagnosis

If you have not yet started exercising, or have quit, you will probably find some of your own excuses here. First, take this simple diagnostic test. Then read the appropriate sections that will help you find ways to overcome your own personal barriers.

The Diagnostic Test

Some of these statements apply to people who have not yet started to exercise and some to people who started but quit. Check off all the statements that apply to you:

• I am afraid exercise will make me look silly. _____ (C)

•I exercised for a while, then stopped when I went on vacation. _____ (A)

•I exercised, but it never felt easy or pleasant. _____(P)

•I will exercise sometime – when I can get my outfit color-coordinated. _____(K)

•I quit because I didn't seem to be improving. _____(R)

•People often laughed at me when I expressed enthusiasm for exercise. _____(S)

•Exercise hurt: My muscles were always sore. _____(P)

•I only exercised because my spouse/doctor wanted me to. _____(W)

•I don't have time. _____(T)

•I think exercise will increase my appetite, and I will put on weight. _____(M)

•I get very tired and/or short of breath when I exercise. _____ (P)

•I felt I would never be as thin (or agile) as the others in the class/group. _____ (R)

•I simply disliked every type of exercise I have tried. _____(W)

•I am afraid I might have a heart attack. _____(M)

•I will exercise when I move closer to my work/when the kids grow up/when I get a different job. _____ (T)

•I don't like to exercise alone. _____(S)

•I can't decide which exercise to try.____(K)

•I used to exercise but stopped when I got sick. ____(A)

•(For women): I am afraid of developing large muscles. ____(M)

•I didn't like the people in the class/group. ____(S)

•I think exercise is a fad, and people will laugh at me for being fashionable. ____(C)

•I would exercise, if the day were an hour longer. ____(T)

•I quit because I never achieved my goals. ____(R)

•I tried running and was sore for a week. ____(P)

•I was just getting started when some relatives came to stay or the weather turned bad or something. ____(A)

The Prescription

Add up the letters, and write the totals here:

T: _____	S: _____	M: ___
W:_____	P: _____	A: _____
R: _____	K: _____	C: _____

If you scored points in any category, read the appropriate section.

The "T" Category: Time Management

If you found yourself checking some "T" statements because you have trouble finding time for exercise, you are not alone. But even if the prospect of extracting 30 minutes out of your day seems daunting (40 if you include the shower), it is probably not impossible. To overcome the notion that there are not enough hours in the day, consider the following four strategies:

1. If possible, add time to your day by exercising early in the morning, when the world is beautiful. You may find that waking 40 minutes or an hour earlier three days a week proves surprisingly easy to manage. Although the hours in bed may be reduced, the quality of sleep may compensate. Regular exercise helps many to fall asleep more easily and sleep more soundly.

2. Double up your activities: exercise and do something else at the same time. For example:

•Read the paper, dictate memos, or watch the television news while you are on your exercise bicycle.

•Listen to tapes of meetings while you walk or jog.

•Arrange to conduct important conversations with family or colleagues while you walk.

3. If you can afford it, hire someone to do something you would otherwise be spending time on (yard work, housecleaning, child watching, car cleaning) and exercise during that time. It's less expensive than a bypass operation (and makes the exercise sessions difficult to forget or skip).

4. Simply make time for exercise. "Im-

possible!" you exclaim? Then complete this exercise. Could you, in an average week, find time to do three of the following? Check which ones you would *not* find excuses to avoid:

__ Stand in the street for half an hour to watch your baseball team parade by after it has won the World Series.

__ Drive to school to talk to your child's teacher.

__ Pick up your son at the airport.

__ Go to a godchild's wedding.

__ Watch your neighbor's slides of his European vacation.

__ Attend a protest meeting about a new high-rise to be built in your neighborhood.

__ Shop for your spouse's anniversary present.

Finished?
Since the chance of all those demands on your time coming up this week is remote, you have probably just liberated three periods of time for exercise. However, don't leave it up to chance; don't rely on finding an empty stretch of time facing you and deciding at the last minute to fill it with exercise. That seldom works. For most people, some preplanning is essential:

• Decide when you will exercise.
• Write it down somewhere, preferably where others can see it and remind you of it, gently, if you forget.

The "A" Category: You Accidentally Quit

Related to the "T" scale is the "A" scale, which was designed to describe those who "accidentally quit." You stopped exercising when you went on vacation, had your mother-in-law visit, attended a conference, or got the flu. It happens all the time, but can be overcome through techniques of relapse anticipation and prevention.

•If you get sick, realize the danger of relapse (which could be more hazardous to your health than your current ailment) and use any part of your brain that can still function to try and avoid it. For example, if you exercise with a friend, telephone to tell him/her what day you can reasonably expect to be back. Don't rush it: Expect to spend a week or so on your own getting back into shape by walking before you resume vigorous exercise. But making that commitment ahead will prevent a slide into inactivity.

•If you are to go on a business trip, find out ahead of time what the exercise facilities are. Business associates or conference organizers are now used to such requests and can fix you up with jogging trails, information on swimming pools, or access to health club facilities.

•Before a vacation, think ahead about its potential for keeping your body in reasonable shape, not necessarily through regular exercise sessions, but as an incidental part of the trip. Try to include at least one activity every day or so that will keep your whole body moving around briskly for 20 minutes or more without stopping. If this activity

---

Eight Ways to Avoid Excuses

1. Be creative about finding time to exercise.

2. Think ahead about possible interruptions to your exercise program and plan ways to minimize or avoid them.

3. Find people you like to exercise with.

4. Set realistic exercise goals.

5. Find an exercise that genuinely entertains you.

6. Don't start an exercise program until you're ready to make a commitment to keep it up.

7. Understand your physical limitations and exercise appropriately.

8. Don't exercise with people who make you feel self-conscious.

doesn't happen to be supplied by a volleyball game, or a game of tennis, or body-surfing, or skiing, or a mountain hike, or sightseeing in a foreign city with no parking places or public transportation, then make a point of adding a fast walk at least once every other day. It won't spoil your vacation, and it will keep your muscles and cardiovascular system primed for your return.

•If social commitments at home, such as visits from relatives, tend to push exercise habits to the back burner (from which they never recover), then plan your strategy well before the visit. A guest should understand that exercise now constitutes an immovable part of your household's routine. If some commitment makes it impossible for you to take part in your normal exercise routine for a week or so, at least plan mini-sessions, or walks, to tide you over.

The "M" Category: Myths

Your barriers are mythological. Exercise need not provoke heart attacks, increase weight, make women look masculine, or do many other things people accuse it of. For myth-management, read "Myths About Exercise" on page 32 and the other chapters on the science and benefits of exercise.

The "S" Category: Social support

If you scored in the "S" category, here's a simple solution to your exercise problems: Find the right kind of people to do it with. Some exercisers relish solitude (and in some cases, as when there is only one exercise bicycle at home, they have little choice). However, if your sport and your schedule can be adapted to include others, your chances of persisting will be greatly enhanced. Exercising with others has a number of additional advantages. It will:
•make time go faster.
•help you go about your exercise in a sensible way, without excesses.

•instill a mildly competitive spirit.

•provide a supportive group of people who will immediately understand your problems, share your aches, and fully appreciate your accomplishments.

Whether you choose to join a formal group or to exercise with one or more friends and colleagues on an informal basis will depend on the sport and your temperament. If your temperament is suited to leadership, then another option opens up: you could ensure your own consistency in exercise by setting up a group yourself! (See the chapter "Exercise with Others" for suggestions.) While you will help others, you will be the main beneficiary, finding it impossible to let your own exercise routine lapse, except at the risk of letting others down.

The "R" Category: Realistic Expectations

If you scored high on the "R" scale, you could use a dose of realism. Either you are expecting too much or too little of yourself, and it is interfering with the reality of what you can actually do.

Most people can improve steadily in both strength and stamina if they stick to their exercise program consistently. Few people, however, can run marathons in their second week. And some should never think of running marathons at all. As you will see from other chapters in this book, even the best natural athletes should start their program gradually; the older you are, and the longer you have been sedentary, the longer it will take to get back in shape. And you will never be as fast/graceful/strong as the athlete 20 - 30 years younger.

By all means set goals, if you are a goal-setting person. For example, decide that one year from now you will enter a 10K race, and will finish it. But if you are new to exercise, don't set your sights on the race next week, or even next month. In the early stages, at least, set goals in terms of time rather than speed or distance. Plan to run/walk/swim an extra ten minutes, at the appropriate heart rate (see the chapter, "Starting to Exercise"): you can't fail.

The "W" Category: Something's Seriously Wrong

"W" responses could signal the need for serious rethinking. Perhaps you tried exercise only because you were ordered to do so; perhaps you have no serious intention of ever trying to enjoy it. Perhaps you have found it, to date, very boring. You are not yet giving up on the whole idea of exercise (if you were, you would probably not be reading this book) but you are thinking about it – and it's certainly a good idea to try to bypass your problems with exercise. Approach the subject from a new angle. Don't think in terms of exercise, but of getting your heart rate up to a respectable beat three times a week for 20 minutes, no matter how you do it.

1. Consider forms of "play" that would genuinely entertain you, and also raise your heart rate, such as:

- roller skating
- ice skating
- skiing (in season)
- surfing
- square dancing
- Scottish country dancing
- soccer/basketball

2. Check out everything you can do safely while watching television or listening to something on headphones (walking, running, stationary cycling, walking up and down your stairs).

3. Think of all the things you could do, and perhaps are doing anyway, that are exercise in disguise: housework or yardwork, walking to lunch, cleaning the car. Upgrade those jobs, if necessary, to make them brisk enough to raise your heart rate to the appropriate range (see page 73) and keep them going for the appropriate length of time. If you can fit in two of those a week, and add one long weekend walk, you can count yourself as an

exerciser, more or less.

The "K" Category: Who Are You Trying To Kid?

If you had "K" responses, you may or may not become a serious exerciser, but it appears that you are not yet ready to risk trying. Your commitment, at most, is wobbly. It may be best to postpone any idea of a regular exercise program right now. Without a serious commitment, you might tend to quit after a few sessions and let that failure inhibit you from trying on later occasions. Better wait until you feel that you have the time, the social support, the right color socks, and a serious intention of starting an exercise program that you will maintain. (Then perhaps start with the suggestions given for the "W" people.)

The "P" Category: Physical Problems

If you checked one or more "P" answers, you quit exercising because of physical difficulties. There is probably no need to give up all idea of exercise (almost everyone with feet — and indeed without them — can do something) but it would be wise to learn what was at the root of your problems.

• If you had any pains in the chest, extreme shortness of breath, or tiredness long after stopping the exercise, tell your doctor.
• If exercise made your

limbs or joints ache, read the chapters on "Starting to Exercise" and "Injuries and Exercise." You probably tried to do too much too soon, with insufficient stretching and perhaps the wrong shoes.

Few people can simply take their bodies out of storage after 20 or 30 years of idleness, dust them off, wind them up, and expect that all the parts will still mesh like a well-tuned machine. Next time, treat your body more gently with a slow start. Expect some minor muscle aches, and expect also to feel physically tired at the end of your exercise session. But don't exercise so vigorously that these symptoms persist, or interfere seriously with the smooth running of your life.

The "C" Category: You Feel Conspicuous

If you checked one or more "C" answers, you feel self-conscious. You feel people are laughing at you for following the exercise fad, or for looking unathletic.

There may, in fact, be no reason for your self-consciousness, but it can be an inhibiting feeling whether justified or not, and it is worth taking seriously. There are various solutions.

•You could exercise at home (for example on an exercise bicycle) until you are too athletic-looking to be laughed at.
•Join a club or class with people in a similar position.
•Walk. To avoid all charges of affectation or faddishness, get a dog to walk with you.

Eventually, exercise should become important enough to overcome the self-consciousness. You honestly won't care what people think, and they will admire and envy you for it.

Conclusion

In a recently concluded project we conducted, one of our more ambitious aims was to get the populations of two California communities on their feet and exercising. Through booklets, newspaper articles, TV spots and programs, worksite contests, neighborhood organizations, fun runs and school-based programs, we urged the populations of Monterey and Salinas to get out there and do something aerobic. Many of them did, and gave us glowing testimonials about the changes exercise had wrought in their lives. But many failed to respond to our urging. Or they responded for a week or so, then went back to their televisions. Even though we had convinced them of the benefits of exercise, we had evidently not given them sufficient tools to overcome the "exercise barriers" in their path.

Our greatest success was with a program that *did* give them the tools to overcome those barriers. This was a self-help "Walking Kit" that got them started slowly, and held their hands every step of the way. We suggest that you follow some of the main principals of that particular program:

1. Make a commitment (to yourself or to others) that you will exercise regularly for a period of at least several weeks.
2. Start slowly: stay well within your capacity.
3. Do all you can to make the experience sociable, enjoyable, and relaxing.
4. Be aware of situations that might lead to a relapse, and take steps to avoid them.

After a few months, if all goes well, you should be hooked and able to look back with astonishment at the sort of wild excuses you once created to avoid this deeply pleasurable activity.

If you start to build your house without a proper concrete foundation, it will never withstand the stress it will soon undergo. Similarly, until you warm-up the body parts you intend to exercise, any activity is too much, too soon.

Injuries

A N D   E X E R C I S E

The leading cause of athletic injuries can be summed up simply: too much, too soon.

At the Stanford Athletic Department's Office of Athletic Training and Sports Medicine, we see 400-500 athletes each day, most with some degree of injury ranging from bruises, strains, and sprains to fractures, dislocation, and nerve injuries. We treat them and explain to the athletes how to avoid aggravating them further. In this chapter we'll show you how, with some preparation, to avoid injury as much as possible.

Know Your Body

If you wanted to erect a house on a vacant piece of property, you'd consult with both a geologist, to make sure the land was stable, and with an architect to design a structure that best utilized the site. Improving your body is no different. Consulting with someone who understands your chosen activity and who can anticipate the long-term effects of the stresses it brings is crucial. Determining these effects is the best way to prevent athletic injuries.

Donald M. Bunce, M.D., and *Standley L. Scott*, R.P.T., A.T.C. Dr. Bunce is an orthopedic surgeon with the Palo Alto Medical Clinic and team physician for the Stanford football team. Mr. Scott is head athletic trainer for all Stanford varsity sports and was on the medical staff of the 1984 Olympic Games.

If you have heart disease, arthritis, diabetes, lower back pain, and other conditions that can prevent you from participating in some activities, your family doctor (a general practitioner) can best determine your medical fitness. If you have had previous bone, muscle or joint injuries, or a postural defect, an orthopedist's advice would be valuable as well.

If you are generally healthy, however, you can determine your physical fitness by performing the self-tests provided in the chapter "Exercise Self-Tests" or by seeing a physical therapist, certified athletic trainer, exercise physiologist, or physical educator. Ideally, these professionals can evaluate your existing condition and recommend programs that will allow you to proceed with your preferred activity.

Physical defects that don't affect the routines of daily living can be magnified greatly once you intensify your level of activity. Running, for instance, magnifies the stress upon your feet five to eight times that of walking. For ballistic sports – anything that involves high-velocity contact with a ball using a bat, a racket, or your foot – it's important to determine whether your body parts can withstand the intensity of impact.

Commonly existing conditions such as leg-length discrepancies (one leg longer than the other), high or low arches, knock-knees or bow-leggedness should all be identified. Special attention should be paid to the patello-femoral joint around the knee-cap, the site of many athletic injuries.

If you have these or other physical deviations, it may be wise to seek advice on alternative athletic activities that may be less stressful for you than the exercise you were planning. Just because everyone else is running doesn't mean that you have to run as well; bicycling, swimming, and walking can be just as beneficial and enjoyable.

Overuse Syndrome

As the body remodels and adapts itself to the stresses of exercise, overuse can occur in almost any body tissue: muscle, joints, or bones. Examples of acute overload injuries include tennis elbow, shin splints, and heal spurs, as well as fractures, dislocations, ligament sprains, and muscle pulls. These injuries are a result of instantaneous stress overload on anatomic structures, resulting in tissue failure. Often the chronic conditions are far more difficult to treat than the acute ones.

In the case of fractures, high-energy stress is often associated with fragmentation of the bone. Lower-energy injuries with a twisting force result in spiral fractures.

Stress fractures are small cracks in the bone cortex caused by repetitive stresses, weight bearing in the lower extremities, and stress on bone from muscle attachments in the upper extremities. They are similar to "fatigue failure" of metal after it has been stressed thousands of times. The difference between bone and metal, of course, is that bone is a dynamic living tissue that has the ability to repair itself.

Seldom do stress fractures lead to complete breaks. Pain often precludes the athlete from continuing at an injurious pace. Stress fractures are extremely common in athletes who are training at high levels and are also very common in the novice exerciser who rapidly increases the frequency, duration, intensity, or biomechanical aspects of a workout. You can develop stress or fatigue fractures in one weekend – again, too much, too soon, too hard – or over the course of a year, even if you're in good shape. Again, bone is dynamic and will not fail if a work-out program is gradual and sensible.

Who is at risk of developing overload injury? Mostly the aged, those previously injured, and those in poor condition. As the aging process occurs, most of the connective tissue of our bodies such as tendons, ligaments, and fascia become weaker and somewhat less elastic, resulting in more frequent overload injuries. Rarely do young athletes pull muscles, develop chronic tendinitis, fasciitis, or bursitis. Women beyond the age of menopause are at high risk of developing osteoporosis, a condition that leads to bones that are more susceptible to stress fractures even with moderate activity. Exercise in moderation, hormone replacement, and sometimes vitamin D, calcium supplements, and fluoride may minimize this risk. Postmenopausal women with osteoporosis may want to seek the advice of an internist or endocrinologist before exercising. Over the last few years more and more attention has been directed toward identifying the high-risk premenopausal runner who has become amenorrheic as a result of running stress to her body, a condition that may lead to early osteoporosis or bone demineralization.

Under normal circumstance, bone is quite durable and like muscle, has the remarkable potential for *remodeling*. That means that bone responds to physical stress or the lack of it, resulting in new bone deposited at sites of stress and reabsorbed from areas of little stress. This concept of remodeling is referred to as Wolfe's Law. It is fundamental to the understanding of basic orthopedics. A dramatic example of Wolfe's Law is the incredible healing and straightening of a child's bone that has been fractured. Initially the healed fracture may be quite angulated, but as months of remodeling pass, the bone eventually returns to its normal shape without a hint of deformity. The younger and more active the individual, the greater the potential for bone remodeling and growth.

A striking example of how bone weakens when it is not stressed is the effect on bone of weightless environments within manned spacecraft. Within a few days, calcium is reabsorbed from the skeletal system. The blood and urine calcium (80 - 100% above pre-flight levels) go up as calcium is leached out of bone, resulting in progressive osteoporosis. It has been estimated that 25% of total body calcium can be lost in one year of space travel (about the time it takes to go from Earth to Mars). Other factors including physical stress, hormones (i.e., estrogen), amount of dietary calcium, intestinal disease, vitamin D, ultraviolet light, and phosphorus are all very important components of healthy bone metabolism. All influence calcium absorption in the body. But physical stress is the only method known to increase bone mass in "normal" individuals, regardless of age. Studies of animals and humans have reported denser, stronger, and usually thicker bones following exercise. More than any other method, exercise can strengthen and maintain healthy bones, countering the effects of injury and aging.

Genetics can also play a role. It has been known for some time that stress fractures are less common in black athletes whose bones may be thicker and stronger than those of whites.

Individuals who have previously been injured are also at risk. Often the rest required to heal a previous injury will result in some degree of muscle atrophy and bone weakness; as a result, those structures may become overloaded when training resumes.

Those in poor condition, therefore, are particularly vulnerable to injury. When an athlete returns to a sport such as skiing and his thigh strength is poor, he is susceptible to muscle fatigue, sometimes resulting in serious injury to the cartilage and ligaments of the knee and the bones of the lower extremities.

Another group at risk are those individuals considered "connective tissue sensitive." These are people who may have early rheumatologic conditions. Recurring joint inflammations and tendinitises are common warning signals.

An Ounce of Prevention

If you start to build your house without a proper concrete foundation, it will never withstand the stress it will soon undergo. Similarly, until you warm up the body parts you intend to exercise, any activity is too much, too soon.

Warm-up readies your body for more intense activity, preparing the nerves, muscles, and joints. It increases the blood flow to the area in question, actually raising its temperature, expanding the tissue, making it more supple and easier to stretch. Blood flow also increases mechanical efficiency by delivering more nutrients and reducing friction. Increased oxygen flow enables the muscles to work harder.

Start a warm-up with jumping jacks or other calisthenics, brisk walking or slow jogging. Generally, when your body breaks into a sweat (usually after about five minutes of activity), you are ready for the next phase of warm-up: stretching.

Stretching should always come midway in the warm-up. If you stretch too soon, your muscles may not be supple enough. Stretching itself should be slow and relaxing, held at the point where you feel tightness within the muscle, never in the joint, for about 30 seconds. All stretches should be done five to ten times and held for about 30 seconds. If there's relaxation of the tension, move an inch or so farther into the stretch. Your breathing should be relaxed and normal and the stretching done slowly. A ballistic or bouncing stretch is not beneficial.

While your particular activity will dictate the best warm-up for you, almost all athletic pursuits involve muscle groups in the calf, the backs of the thighs (hamstrings), the back, and the abdomen. These areas almost always need to be warmed for optimal flexibility. Following are suggestions for warming up these muscle groups.

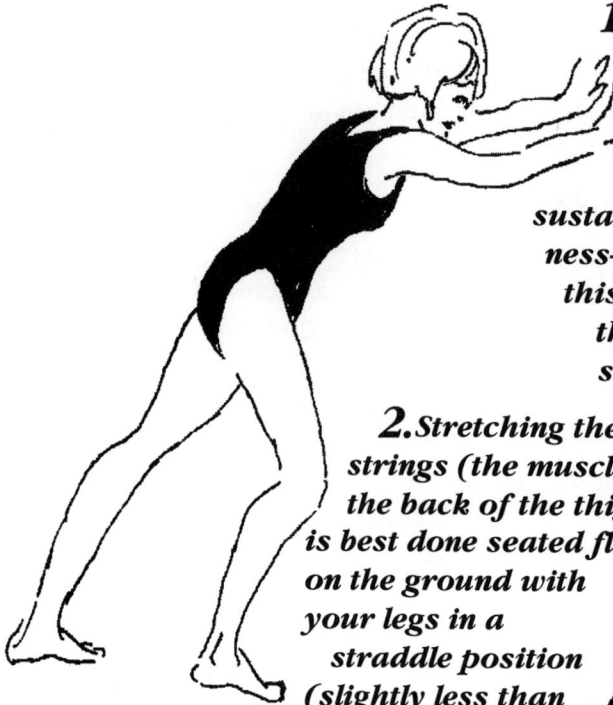

1. *Stretching the calf is best done by placing your hands against a wall or tree, with your foot flat and your leg straight. Lean forward with a slow, sustained motion to the point of tightness— and then let your leg relax. Do this first with the knee straight and then with the knee slightly bent to stretch all the necessary muscles.*

2. *Stretching the hamstrings (the muscles on the back of the thigh) is best done seated flat on the ground with your legs in a straddle position (slightly less than a 90° spread). Alternately reach both hands toward one foot, always keeping the knee straight and the foot pointed upward, and then reach forward between your legs. This position spares tension to the nerves and ligaments connected to the lower back.*

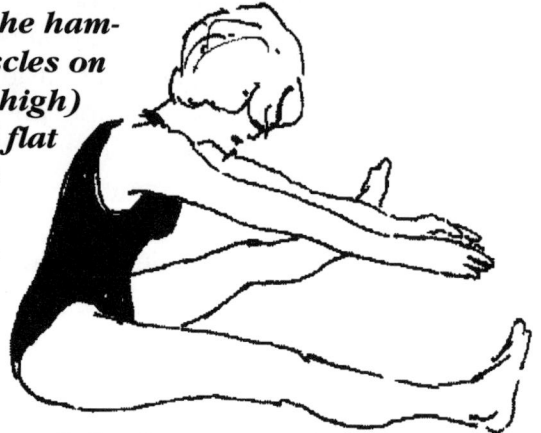

3. *The best way to stretch the back for most people is to lie on your back with your knees bent and your feet flat on the floor. Grab your knees and squeeze them up to your*

chest. Hold them there for ten seconds or so, and then slowly lower your knees back to the floor, one leg at a time, always keeping your knees bent.
Repeat ten times.

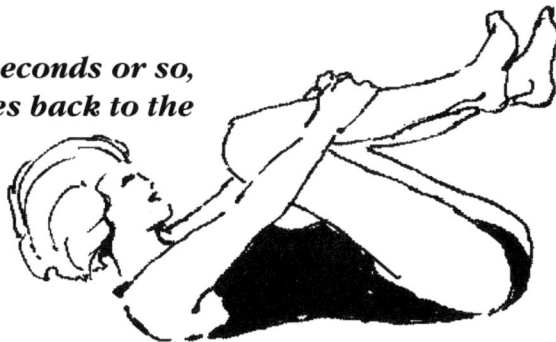

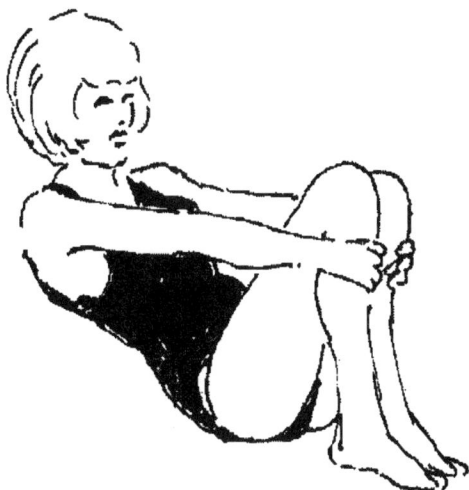

4. You can best warm up your abdominals by exercising rather than stretching them. Lie in the back warm-up position, then curl your shoulder blades up. Abdominal warm-ups stretch the lower back and stabilize the pelvis, helping to avoid lower back strain.

The third stage of warm-up actually involves rehearsing your planned athletic activity at a less intense level (e.g tennis serves at 50% rather than "aces").

To prevent injury, a gradual "cool-down" at the end of your exercise is just as crucial as a pre-exercise warm-up. Gradually decrease the intensity of your activity to allow your system to return to a normal resting state slowly, rather than abruptly. Spend five or ten minutes, after you've exercised, slowly walking or stretching to allow your body to remove lactic acid and other chemical waste products of exercise from your muscles, rather than allowing them to settle there.

A gradual instead of abrupt decrease in blood flow after exercise allows the continual exchange of nutrients and waste products. If the metabolites of exercise are trapped in your muscles, soreness may result, since the oxygen in your muscles may not be efficiently replenished. Abruptly ending exercise can also cause dizziness or fainting.

Myths of Warm-Up

As exercise has become more a part of people's lives for longer periods of time, health care professionals have been able to study the long-term effects of exercise and identify some of the most dangerous myths of warm-up.

For instance, the long-advocated duck walk – waddling on your haunches – is actually detrimental to your knees. Any time you flex your knees, particularly with your full weight on them, you risk damaging them. Also, the hurdler's stretch – sitting with one leg straight in front and the other bent back at your side – puts undue pressure on the hip joint and the medial side of the knees.

Straight leg raises – lying flat on your back and lifting both legs – puts stress on the back and doesn't strengthen the muscles you might think. Even touching your toes while standing doesn't stretch the hamstrings adequately and should be avoided because of possible stress on the back.

Equipment-Related Problems

Your clothes are equipment; your shoes are equipment. And unless you've prepared them properly, you're not yet ready to exercise.

Dressing smart is easy. Judge the weather and don't allow yourself either to be overheated or overcooled. Remember that your body needs some method of evaporation, even in cold weather.

The most common equipment-related injury stems from a bad shoe fit. The mechanics of the foot and the entire leg are such that, improperly equipped, they can contribute to injuries – even those that are not foot-related. For instance, women are more susceptible to lower-extremity injuries than men because of the shape of the pelvis and the way their legs angulate; the stresses on their hips, their knees and, as a result, their feet contribute to problems that incorrect shoes only aggravate.

If you have a pre-exercise physical examination, it should include your feet, in particular the arches. Lack of arch support can lead to significant injury. One common foot motion is called pronation, which is the flattening of the inside of the foot under weight. Pronation and hyperpronation can cause a chain reaction of problems all the way up the leg to the back, but good shoe fit can correct them.

If your athletic program is going to include home exercise equipment, mention this to your health care professional. There's a wide variety of home equipment, most of which is very good. But again, any pre-existing conditions you have need to be identified. You may not fit into a particular machine the way a normal or unaffected body would. A previous injury that has resulted in stiffness, tightness, or lack of motion coupled with the configuration of the equipment may cause you to find yourself sitting or lying down in an unnatural position that creates additional problems for you. A previous injury to your patello-femoral joint, for instance, may preclude you from straightening your knee against resistance, as some equipment requires.

Use the concept of *progressive resistance exercise* with a machine. Increase the intensity of your exercise incrementally; when ten repetitions come easily, increase the number of reps, or the poundage. If you ease into a machine's use, and don't overdo, it's not likely that you can injure yourself. Most of the machines available are safe (see also the chapter, "The Science of Exercise").

Identifying An Injury

If you do sustain an injury, you need to know how to identify it and keep it from getting worse.

Defining an injury is difficult because you're dealing with something as subjective as pain. Some people can tune out pain, others will deny it. The important thing is to discern the difference between pain and discomfort. You have to be able to differentiate between the feeling of having worked hard and a consistently recurring pain that comes on every repetition of a motion; the latter is a good warning sign that something's awry.

Pain can also communicate that more rest is needed between intense workouts, that you should go more slowly, or that you haven't recovered from a previous injury. An interval of rest is just as important as the exercise itself. Your soreness must subside before you exercise again; it's crucial that you don't try to work through the pain.

The method we often use with young athletes is to have them describe the quality of pain and rate it on a scale of one to ten. Muscle soreness can manifest itself at rest, after you've exercised, and that's no cause for concern. But if you have an aching pain keeping you awake or even awakening you from sleep, it should be investigated. If you find yourself taking an undue amount of pain medication, too, seek professional medical advice. Dizziness, fainting, chest pain or pressure, numbness, or tingling should also be checked.

Another warning sign is crepitus, which is almost any sound emitted by a body part that's not working correctly. Squeaking, grating, or rubbing all qualify; there's even "snowball crepitus," resembling the sound of walking on snow, which is usually a sign of tendinitis (inflammation of the tendon).

When you exercise regularly, you must acknowledge that your capacities do decrease with age. Realize too that an area that's been injured is going to have a lower tolerance for stress.

Common Types of Injuries

Under no circumstances do we recommend self-diagnosis of pain and injury. You can suffer concomitant injuries – for example, neuritis while you have muscle strain, while you have a sprain, while you have a bruise, while you have a stress fracture – and it takes a health professional to determine the true mechanism of injury. Nevertheless, there are common injuries you should be able to recognize in order to avoid aggravating them further.

Strains

Probably the most common type of injury, strains are damage to the muscle or the muscles' components from stretching, ripping, or tearing of its connective tissue. (Tendinitis, for instance, occurs where the muscle attaches to the bone.) There may not be visible signs of muscle strain, but for the most part it hurts to stretch and contract a muscle that's been strained. Stretching it will increase the temperature and make the pain more tolerable, but the ache will return at rest.

Tennis elbow is one of the most common types of strain, usually the result of ballistic maneuvers in racket sports. It appears in the group of muscles known as the forearm extensors. It can be avoided with isometric wrist extensions (pressing the wrist against an immovable object for six to eight seconds). Because it can involve nerve irritation, tendinitis may require injected medicine for treatment.

Another common strain is plantar fasciitis, a muscle strain relating to the mechanics of the foot. The bowstring supporting the long arch of the foot can be excessively stretched, causing pain when it bears weight. A common running injury, it's worsened by running uphill on your toes, or even bouncing on your toes. Anytime you concentrate force on a small area where it can't dissipate to other joints, undue stress occurs. Untreated, plantar fasciitis can lead to heel spurs, which may require surgery or injected medicine to correct.

One of the easiest injuries to occur – and one of the least understood – is shin splint syndrome. Shin splint syndrome is actually a general term covering half a dozen theories for pain in the lower leg. It can refer to muscle strains or perhaps irritation of the membrane over the bone. Shin splints occur when the intensity of activity is suddenly increased before the muscles involved are properly conditioned, and they can usually be prevented by stretching, good flexibility, and proper footwear. Unfortunately, shin splints can be the precursor to a condition called compartment syndrome, which left unchecked can eventually cause crippling vascular damage and/or foot problems.

Sprains

Also very common, sprains relate to joints as strains relate to muscles. In a sprain, tearing or stretching occurs in the connective tissue of the joints, such as the ligaments. Swelling and even deformity often indicate a sprain.

Treatment of Injuries: The RICE Principle

There are times, of course, when self-treatment is perfectly acceptable. Treated correctly, minor injuries heal without developing into major problems. You simply need to follow some common tenets regarding the use of heat and cold therapy.

Most importantly, heat should never be applied to a new injury. It's tempting to ease the soreness with heat from a bath, water bottle, lamp, or heating pad, but if an injury is swollen, it may indicate internal bleeding and swelling. Increasing heat, just as in warm-ups, brings more blood to the injury, which increases the bleeding and swelling. It may be comfortable, but it's not beneficial.

The acronym to remember for new injuries – whether strains, sprains, or bruises – is *RICE; rest, ice, compression* (such as an elastic bandage), and *elevation.*

When you apply ice to a body part, it decreases the blood flow to the area via vasoconstriction. In this process, the capillaries constrict, and their walls become less permeable, allowing less blood to flow into the tissues. Cold therapy makes the battlefield smaller, so to speak, thus reducing the area of hypoxic injury (i.e., injury from lack of oxygen). Ice lowers the metabolic rate so that less oxygen is needed and the proximate area isn't damaged. It is also an anesthetic, numbing pain and reducing muscle spasm.

As with all facets of injury prevention, there are rules to follow with ice; it can, after all, be dangerous if applied incorrectly. Always apply cold with an insulating layer – a towel, a plastic bag, or even submersion – but never with a stationary, static application. Ice the injury for 20 minutes, then let it warm for about one hour; then repeat. Another alternative is ice massage – essentially rubbing ice over the injured body part – but that should be done for no more than 12 minutes at a time.

For a significant injury, continue the cycle of 20 minutes of cold treatment and 60 minutes without treatment for 24 to 36 hours. Only after that period of time is it safe to apply heat, and then as locally as possible; sitting up to your neck in a tub of hot water is not going to help your ankle. Also remember that moist heat works far better than dry heat; thus, a moist hot pack is more therapeutic than an infrared lamp.

Finally, avoid balms or ointments that may have a derivation of the word "heat" in their brand name. As skin irritants that only give the sensation of warmth and comfort, they are not true therapeutic heat as they don't increase the blood flow to the area, or its temperature.

In Conclusion

If you follow this progression — examine your physical and medical capabilities, adequately warm up and cool down, sense your body's gradual advancement without overextending its limits, and care for the aches and discomforts you experience— you can logically hope to avoid undue injury and pain. The key word is *gradual*: healthy body parts are developed, carefully using exercise training techniques that emphasize slow, gradual, and systematic progressions. This approach will help individuals prevent injuries which are typically associated with the "Overuse Syndrome."

Injury Avoidance Checklist

1. Understand any special conditions your body may have, and exercise appropriately.

2. Include warm-up and cool-down as part of your exercise routine.

3. Make sure your shoes fit properly and your clothes allow evaporation of sweat.

4. Know the difference between pain and discomfort.

5. Don't try to diagnose an injury yourself.

6. Treat minor injuries using the RICE principle: rest, ice, compression (such as elastic bandage), and elevation.

In fact, even though post-myocardial infarction patients have suffered a life-threatening event, by starting an exercise program they may soon feel better than at any other time in their lives.

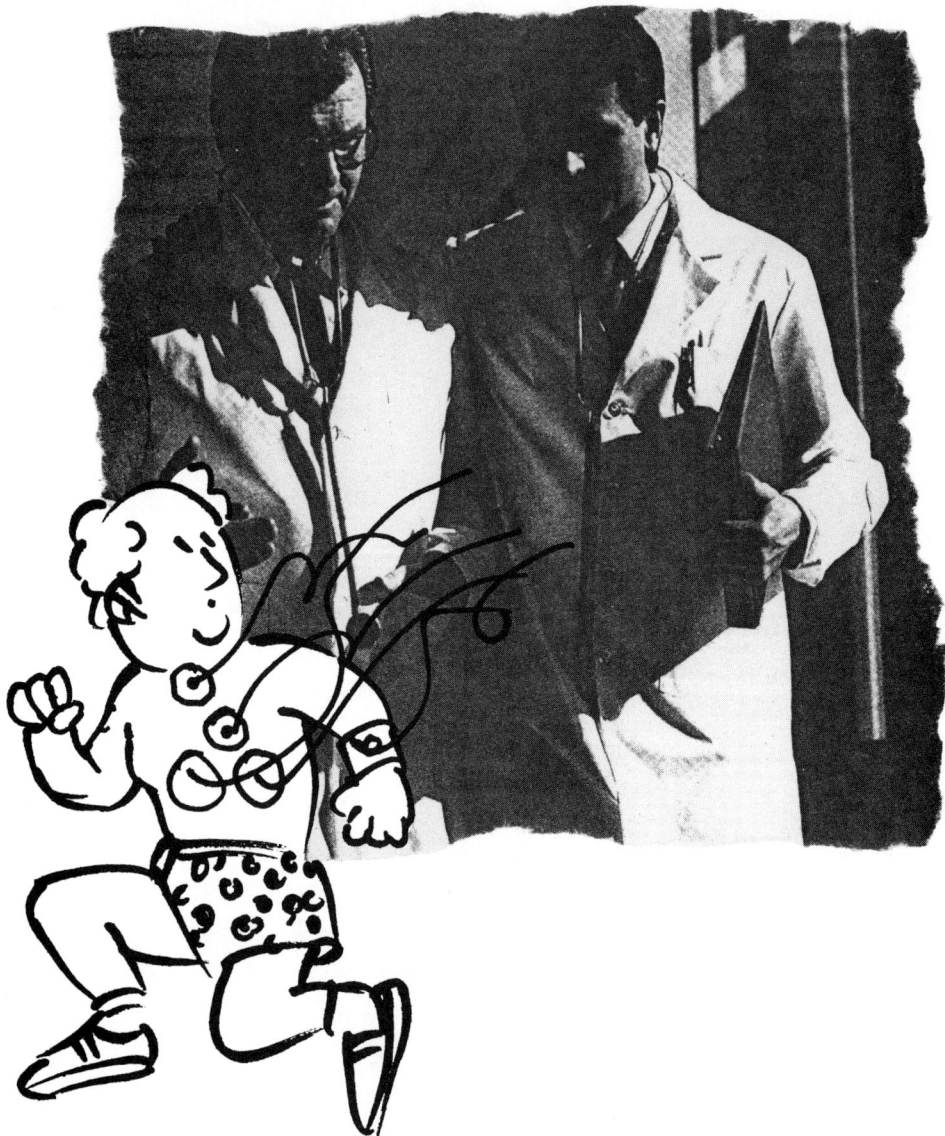

Heart Attack

I n the past, people who had suffered a heart attack (myocardial infarction) were confined to bed for six weeks and were frequently unable to resume exercise until at least three months after the event. However, during the last decade, significant advances in medical research have brought a much fuller understanding of the processes involved in recovery from a myocardial infarction.

We know that by three weeks after an attack, the heart has already healed sufficiently to sustain considerable exercise. By six weeks, a firm scar tissue has formed, and most patients can be assured that they can resume their normal lives and return to their previous level of exercise, or even exceed it, without undue concern. Of course, to resume normal activity safely and as soon as possible after a heart attack requires a careful systematic evaluation and management.

Nancy Houston-Miller, R.N., *Robert F. DeBusk*, M.D., *C. Barr Taylor*, M.D. Ms. Miller is program nurse coordinator, Stanford Cardiac Rehabilitation Program (SCRP), and community outreach director for the Health Promotion Resources Center. Dr. DeBusk is professor of medicine, Stanford Medical School, and director, SCRP. Dr. Taylor is associate professor of psychiatry (clinical), Stanford Medical School, and director of behavioral science, SCRDP.

Benefits of Exercise for Heart Attack Patients

The benefits of exercise for patients suffering a myocardial infarction are similar to those experienced by the general population (see the chapter, "Benefits of Exercise"). Exercise helps reduce weight, blood pressure, and stress. Moreover, exercise may increase the beneficial type of cholesterol, HDL, especially in those who undertake exercise on a regular basis. We have also found that exercise helps post-myocardial infarction patients cut down on the number of cigarettes they smoke and may help people stop altogether, an important link in risk factor reduction.

Regular exercise also has benefits that are of special significance to post-myocardial infarction patients, including psychological improvement and the reduced demand for oxygen by the heart as it becomes more efficient.

The psychological needs of patients following an acute myocardial infarction are understandable. Many are anxious and uncertain about their ability to resume work and other customary activities. They may be depressed if they are unduly restricted from these activities. Counseling about the safety of returning to a normal lifestyle including exercise can be of enormous psychological benefit to the patient and spouse. As patients become more physically active through exercise, and see their own capabilities return, depression tends to dissipate, and their anxiety is relieved.

Exercise also causes physiological changes that can enhance a patient's feeling of well-being. As the heart rate decreases from exercise training, the heart muscle becomes more efficient. Those patients suffering symptoms of angina (lack of oxygen to the heart muscle) often find that their symptoms are alleviated and may in fact disappear. As a result, patients become able to carry out physical activities without feeling significant discomfort.

Eligibility for Exercise - Treadmill Testing

Approximately 1.5 million people suffer myocardial infarctions each year. Of these, approximately 40 - 50% are eligible for exercise based on the fact they are at "low risk" for reinfarction or death and have no limiting medical or musculoskeletal conditions.

As early as five days after a heart attack, clinical and historical characteristics can identify some patients as being at "low risk." If the treadmill test at two to three weeks after the heart attack shows an absence of *myocardial ischemia* (oxygen deprivation to the heart) and *left ventricular dysfunction* (poor pumping function), the patient can generally be classified as "low risk." This test is of great value. It gives realistic expectations about their ability to resume customary activities and helps define their medical prognosis.

While "high-risk" patients often require further diagnostic studies and treatments, the "low-risk" group can be immediately cleared for exercise training, which will in itself increase their confidence in their ability to engage in a number of other activities, such as rapid walking, cycling, yard work, and sexual relations. This gradual resumption of customary activity brings about additional physical and psychological benefits.

For those whose risk is in fact low, "symptom-limited exercise testing" (as the treadmill test is known) offers a passport to freedom that was unheard of for heart attack patients a generation ago. It measures the heart's capacity to tolerate a wide variety of stresses encountered during customary activities. And it can be used to reassure patients in the "low-risk" category that their risk of dying from a heart attack is low – less than 2% a year. That increased confidence can itself be a major factor in ensuring recovery.

The Exercise Prescription After Heart Attack

Within three months of a heart attack, a low-risk patient's exercise capacity is equivalent to that of a healthy male between the ages of 50 and 59. The prescribed exercise program is similar to that recommended for any beginner. Individual walking, cycling, or jogging programs are prescribed to exercise the large muscle groups of the legs for 20 - 30 minutes a day. Like the general public, post-myocardial infarction patients exercise at 70 - 85% of the peak heart rate, although recent studies have shown that exercise at lower intensities (60% of maximum heart rate) will also enhance their cardiovascular health.

In the past, patients sustaining a myocardial infarction typically exercised in a group setting under medical supervision. However, the ability to identify very low-risk patients has enabled us to reevaluate that approach. In a randomized trial of clinically low-risk patients, the Stanford Cardiac Rehabilitation Program assigned some to exercise at home, while some remained in a supervised group. Those who exercised at home were given individualized guidelines for exercise intensity based on a tread-mill evaluation at three weeks after the heart attack. They also used heart rate monitors to help them stay within the prescribed range of intensity. From week to week they were monitored during exercise sessions by means of an electrocardiogram trans-mitted over the telephone. We found this at-home exercise train-ing to be just as effective – and just as safe – as supervised group training in increasing functional capacity. No training-related cardiac events were noted. Additional studies without the elabo-rate monitoring equipment have further substantiated the safety of home training for these low-risk patients.

At-home exercise allows post-myocardial infarction pa-tients to benefit from exercise. Currently, medically supervised group programs are available to no more than 15 - 20% of the post-myocardial infarction population. In some cases, there may not be sufficient funds to support a program, while in other cases, particularly in small communities, there may not be enough patients to justify forming a group. Home exercise training provides a way to meet the needs of the 40 - 50% of low-risk patients who don't have access to medically supervised group programs.

Safety Precautions

As with any exercise program, the importance of safety needs to be underscored. A few patients, for example, tend to overexert and deny resulting symptoms. Post-myocardial infarction patients involved in exercise must be in touch with their body's feelings, using self-monitoring skills to be alert for any warning signals such as chest discomfort, undue fatigue, shortness of breath, and development of an irregular pulse or heart beat – symptoms which may mean that the patient should stop exercising and seek medical attention. The ability to recognize a change in symp-toms and to seek medical attention is critical to ensuring the safety of continued exercise.

In our program we do our best to ensure the safety of patients through our selection process and the development of patients's self-monitoring skills. To a great extent, however, safety is in the hands of the individual patients who must regulate the intensity of exercise within individually prescribed limits, and who must always discontinue exercise sessions if they do not feel well. Often, patients involved in supervised-exercise programs have had cardiac events simply because they failed to exercise within their prescribed heart rate limits. For this reason, patients must carefully monitor their heart rates while exercising by checking their pulses. Any patient who is unable to comply with a carefully developed exercise prescription based on heart rate may place himself at high risk for a serious cardiac event.

As a final safety measure, all patients should be given repeat treadmill exercise tests at yearly intervals to determine any change in their cardiovascular status. This treadmill test not only provides information about the clinical status of the patient, but becomes a good motivator for continued exercises.

Enhancing the Future

Although interruptions in their schedules may cause some patients to lapse in their exercise, many patients become truly committed to it and are so thoroughly convinced of its benefits that physical activity becomes a way of life. While "high-risk" individuals will continue to exercise in medically supervised groups such as those offered through hospitals, community colleges, and YMCAs, "low-risk" patients can and should be offered an individualized approach to exercise that may include home training.

The well-being of more and more heart attack patients will improve dramatically as they are offered exercise opportunities. In fact, even though post-myocardial infarction patients have suffered a life-threatening event, by starting an exercise program, they may soon feel better than at any other time in their lives.

Repeated, chronic activation of your "flight or fight" response can over time make you more vulnerable to disease and disability.

Stress

I n one way or another, stress contributes to most physical or emotional disorders. It may initiate some problems like skin eruptions or exacerbate others like high blood pressure. And emotionally, sustained stress is associated with anxiety and depression. It interferes with our ability to concentrate, to make decisions, to relax, and to get along with our colleagues and family.

We don't know exactly how stress plays a part in these problems. We do know, however, that there are multiple facets of stress, including positive ones.

Think about the last wedding you participated in or the last vacation you embarked on. While joyous occasions, they no doubt involved some stress (who hasn't remarked upon their return that "I need a vacation to recuperate from my vacation"?). Positive stress can excite us to new levels of creativity and energy. It is termed "eustress" to distinguish it from "distress." It's the latter, when it's unremitting, chronic, or uncontrollable, that becomes dangerous.

Abby King, Ph.D., and
C. Barr Taylor, M.D.
Dr. King is research associate, SCRDP, and has been a consultant to the U.S. Department of Health and Human Services and the Center for Disease Control. Dr. Taylor is associate professor of psychiatry (clinical) at Stanford Medical School and director of Behavioral Science, SCRDP.

Where Stress Comes From, Where It Goes

Left over in our bodies from prehistoric days is the "flight or fight" response to the threat of perceived threats and demands. Its presence allowed us to either escape or eventually conquer threats of mastodons and saber-toothed tigers. Today, it's not so easy to fight or flee employers, rebellious children, and surly civil servants.

Instead we live with the anxiety they create, and our bodies respond by getting ready for battles that never take place. Repeated, chronic activation of your "flight or fight" response can over time make you more vulnerable to disease and disability.

Moreover, if you use caffeine, tobacco or alcohol to try to reduce stress, your health may be further endangered. Even resorting to consumption of convenient, high-fat, fast foods – because you're too revved up to slow down and prepare a well-balanced meal – may tend to damage your health in the long run.

What we perceive as stressful varies from person to person, as well as within the same person across time. Once you understand your own personal stress reactions and causes, you can learn to manage them. Like exercise, stress management, if it is to be successful, needs to be tackled regularly until it becomes a habit.

Research by behavioral scientists at Stanford and elsewhere has suggested that problem-solving strategies are effective in helping people manage stress in their lives. The problem-solving approach has five basic steps that include:

1) Identify your major signs of stress. Take a moment to think about this and use the chart to the left to help you.

Signs of Stress List

Physical	Mental-Emotional	Behavioral
Increased heart rate	Difficulty concentrating	Increased arguing
Changes in breathing	Distractibility	Increased crying
Muscle tension	Narrowing of focus	Social withdrawal
Tension headaches	Anxiety, nervousness	Sleep changes
Stomach/GI problems	Moodiness, depression	Changes in appetite
Cold hands and/or feet	Self-deprecatory thoughts	Poor performance
Sweaty palms	Irritability, anger	Changes in health habits
Hives, skin eruptions	Other:_____	Voice changes
Increased perspiration	Other:_____	Other:_____
Fatigue		Other:_____
Shakiness		
Other:_____		
Other:_____		

2) Define your problem situations.

This can be accomplished through self-monitoring and the next chart can help you with this.

Daily Stress and Tension Log					
Stress or Tensions Felt	Date and Time	*** Stress Rating	Where? Doing What? With Whom?	Thoughts/ Feelings	Response to Stress

*** Rating Scale: 1-7 (1 - very relaxed 7 - very stressed)

3) Develop possible solutions.

These help you avoid, alter, or adapt to the situation.

4) Pick a strategy and put it into action.

Behavioral "contracts" similar to the following examples can help with this stage.

Behavioral Contract

Responsibilities:

For the next two weeks, as an aid to managing my stress levels, I will do the following:

1. Let my coworkers know the specific times during the day when I will be unavailable for questions or other interruptions.   As an additional prompt, I will place a "do not disturb" sign on my door during those times.

2. Defer any questions/problems during those designated periods to my coworker, Jane Doe, as we have previously agreed.

This work plan will be evaluated by my recording number of interruptions during those times.

3. Go for a walk after work at least three times during each week, as a way of helping me to unwind.

My walking goal will be evaluated by me noting number of times walked on my home calendar.

These goals will be reevaluated in two weeks.

*Signed:*_____

*Work Helper (Jane Doe):*_____

*Home Helper:*_____

*Date:*_____

*Date:*_____

---

5) Evaluate how you are doing.

Is my stress-reduction strategy working? If so, how? If not, why not? Do I need a different strategy?

For some people exercise is a useful stress-reduction strategy.

Exercise and Stress Response

According to a growing body of evidence, physical activity may be able to counter the negative emotional effects of stress and be a significant aid in stress management.

William P. Morgan, a renowned sports psychologist, has documented that world-class athletes score below the general population on traits associated with anxiety, depression, anger, fatigue, and confusion, and above the general population on vigor. Similar results have been observed in nonathletic individuals who have been involved in a regular exercise program.

There is other evidence that exercise can reduce depression. In a Stanford study on post-cardiac patients, 13% of the men in the sample were moderately to severely depressed after their heart attack. Those who were placed on a regimen involving medically supervised gym training showed a significant reduction on one measure of depression, compared to a control group. Of course, it is hard to generalize from this type of study; the fact that the men found themselves fit enough to exercise at all could have been responsible for much of their improvement.

However, other studies support the hypothesis that physical activity and exercise probably help alleviate some of the symptoms associated with mild to moderate depression. There is also evidence that exercise can provide a beneficial adjunct to substance abuse programs, reducing symptoms of anxiety and improving self-image.

In fact, the question of whether or not exercise has an anti-depressive, calming effect may depend on the setting and the circumstances. At the very least, physical activity can provide valuable "time out" during which the normal stresses of the day will cease. It can also enhance this time out by enabling people to enjoy positive soothing experiences such as music, nature, the weather, or good conversation — which may be as beneficial as the exercise itself.

In addition, exercise can have the benefit of making people feel they are doing something positive for their health —

that they are taking charge. This alone can be useful in stress reduction, and for psychological well-being in general. Moreover, there is evidence that aerobic training may be of value in reducing the physiological effects of stress.

In a study conducted through the Veterans Administration Medical Center at Jackson, Miss., in collaboration with the University of Mississippi, men with somewhat elevated blood pressure were observed as they underwent the stress of an exciting video game. Those men who had undergone aerobic exercise training showed a rise in pressure that was significantly smaller than that experienced by the men who had no such training. In other words, it appears that, for at least some people, exercise may lessen the damage that could otherwise be caused by the sudden rises in blood pressure resulting from unavoidable stress. Continued research will elucidate further the relationship between exercise and the physical responses to stress.

The Other Side of the Coin

There is, however, a "down" side. Under certain circumstances, an exercise session may be far from serene, and may even increase the level of anxiety.

A simple problem can be that of scheduling. In an ideal world, you would find an otherwise free stretch of time in which to take your exercise, or would cancel a less important activity in order to make room for it. In other words, you would choose to jog instead of watching the news before dinner; or you would take some morning exercise instead of doing the crossword puzzle.

For many people, it doesn't work like that. Instead of replacing something on their schedule, they add exercise to it. If the schedule is already full, the addition of exercise to it may well produce considerable anxiety. "How am I ever going to get this work done in time to get out of here?" "Should I have said 5:30 instead of 5:00?" "Suppose I get stuck in traffic?" "Suppose we get to the racquetball place and don't get a court?" "Suppose

I lose?" "I'll be home late again and Karen will be mad." . . . If you add to these tensions a form of activity that is competitive, exercise may become about as soothing as a plane wreck.

For some people, even the less competitive forms of activity such as running or bicycling can produce great tension under certain circumstances. A crowded running track or a bicycle lane on a bus route can bring out depressingly hostile sides to the nature of otherwise docile people.

In general, however, physical activity is an excellent method for helping you cope with the stress of your life. It provides an opportunity to leave daily stresses behind and focus your energies and thoughts on something positive. The physical and psychological benefits of exercise include a decrease in tension and anxiety as well as, for some, an increase in feelings of well-being. Among the most notable physical benefits are an increased capacity to do work, which may be of substantial benefits to individuals whose careers involve ongoing challenges.

*T*he best guess at this time is that exercise does have a modest, independent blood-pressure-lowering effect.

Exercise &

"High" blood pressure is now somewhat lower than it used to be. Blood pressure that 10 years ago might have been considered "within normal limits" is now, thanks to long-term studies, looked at as risky. Quite simply, we have found that even mild elevation of pressure increases the risk of heart disease and stroke.

The change in physicians' attitude towards the systolic pressure (the high number recorded when your heart is actually beating) has been particularly dramatic. Whereas not long ago it was thought respectable to have a systolic pressure of your age plus 100, that is now considered much too high after the age of 20. Current recommendations are that the systolic should ideally stay at or below 120 for life, and that anything over 140 should be carefully evaluated by a physician.

Stephen P. Fortmann, M.D., *is associate director, SCRDP and assistant professor, department of medicine, Stanford Medical School. Dr. Fortmann serves on the coordinating committee for community demonstration studies of the National Heart, Lung and Blood Institute, Washington, D.C.*

Meanwhile, diastolic pressure (the low number, indicating the pressure between beats) should ideally stay at 80 or below for life. Most physicians now express concern with any diastolic pressure above 90 or 95.

In most cases, doctors tend to prescribe drugs when presented with any pressure that is consistently higher than 150/100, especially if the patient has elevated cholesterol or smokes cigarettes. Increasingly, I am glad to say, physicians will suggest changes in lifestyle before they resort to drugs. These measures often include:

- a reduction in salt, which can have a distinct effect on those susceptible to it
- a reduction in weight
- a reduction in caffeine and alcohol, both of which can raise pressure in certain individuals
- a less stressful existence
- exercise

Why exercise? Because even though we don't know precisely how (or even whether) exercise has an independent effect on blood pressure levels, it seems to help reduce them. In many cases, the main benefit of exercise will come from its effect on weight, or perhaps on stress. And there is now some evidence that exercise alone does indeed have some independent effect on pressure.

The connection between exercise and blood pressure is complex, and much of the research on this issue has unfortunately ignored this. Indeed, blood pressure is affected by so many factors that good research studies must have a control group to ensure that changes in blood pressure can be attributed to exercise, and not to other factors involved, such as weight loss.

One study which did make good use of a control group was performed by Dr. Steven Blair and his colleagues at the Institute for Aerobics Research in Dallas. Studying 56 young people with mild hypertension, he picked 12 at random to act as controls. The 44 others participated in three 60-minute walk/jog sessions a week for a period of 16 weeks. Although their weight did not change, their average blood pressure declined from 146/94 to 134/87. In the control group, whose weight also remained stable, the systolic pressure also dropped from an average of 145 to 138, but the group's diastolic pressure did not decline during the 16-week trial (indeed it went up by an average of three points). This finding illustrates the need for control groups quite well and means that the exercise program appeared to have a more significant effect on the diastolic than on the systolic pressure.

Several other controlled studies do exist, and the best guess at this time is that exercise does have a modest, independent blood-pressure-lowering effect. When this is added to its effect on weight and stress, exercise's total benefit to blood pressure control becomes considerably greater.

Exercise and Weight

Excess weight plays an important role in blood pressure; for many individuals, it is more beneficial to reduce weight than to cut down on sodium (although in an ideal world, they do both).

When we look at whole populations, the role of sodium is plainly an important one. Those populations with a high-sodium diet have much higher average blood pressures than those whose diet is relatively low in salt. Some individuals, however, may not show major reductions in blood pressure in response to a reduction in salt, although salt restriction is worth trying. But almost all individuals will reduce their pressure if they lose weight, usually at the rate of about one point of systolic pressure for each one or two pounds lost. And exercise is a vital component in almost all successful weight-loss programs.

In addition to the obvious fact that exercise uses up calories, and therefore allows you to eat a reasonable amount of food while losing weight, it influences other important factors in weight loss: the type of weight that is lost (whether fat or muscle) and a person's basic resting metabolism.

Any weight-loss program that relies for its effectiveness on a reduction in calories alone will remove surplus flab from your frame, but it will also diminish your stock of lean muscle tissue. Since muscle tissue uses up more calories than flab, its loss will make it harder for you to keep the weight off when you go back to a normal way of eating.

On the other hand, if part or all of your weight loss comes from an increase in exercise, you will be building more muscle tissue, and that will increase your body's capacity to use up incoming calories without going on a starvation diet.

Some exciting research in the last decade by my colleague Peter Wood and others (see the chapter, "Diet and Exercise") has indicated that a systematic program of aerobic exercise can speed up the basic metabolic rate, or BMR. Thanks to a hopped-up BMR, the "trained" person will use up more calories than the untrained, even while resting.

Related to this, perhaps, is the discovery that the "appetite alarms" in the exercised person are more reliable than in the non-exerciser. A program of systematic exercise may increase the likelihood that when you feel hungry, you are hungry; and that will obviously make it somewhat easier to resist the snacks that are the nemesis of most would-be weight-losers. There is evidence that moderate exercise, such as a brisk walk before dinner, can actually reduce the appetite.

Stress

The role of stress in hypertension is hard to pin down, but there is enough hard evidence to indicate that it can certainly be a factor. It definitely can boost blood pressure temporarily. The shot of adrenalin that comes with any sudden excitement increases blood pressure in addition to speeding up the heart rate as it prepares us for a "fight or flight" response. In normotensives – people whose blood pressure is not high – the pressure goes back down again as soon as the "emergency" is over.

Some investigators believe that chronic stress helps create changes in the body that produce sustained blood pressure elevation. Several studies have shown small reductions in blood pressure with regular stress reduction efforts. A program that reduces stress, be it meditation, yoga, or (you've guessed it) exercise, may make a useful addition to a program for the control of high blood pressure.

How does exercise reduce stress? Partly through some very fancy biochemical activity in the brain. Systematic exercise can apparently increase the supply of endorphins in the bloodstream, which in turn can act as natural tranquilizers (and produce the "runner's high" that has so often, and lyrically, been described). Endorphins can also account for the apparent reduction in stress levels that many of us experience when we are exercising.

Even without a biochemical explanation, however, there are ample reasons why exercise has a beneficial effect on stress levels. When you exercise, you are away from everyday pressures, able to let your mind roam free; you feel more in control of your body and destiny. If you exercise outside, you are able to appreciate some of the natural beauty around you. If you exercise with a friend or spouse, you have a perfect setting for low-key conversation and companionship. All of this helps to control or counteract stress.

Alcohol, Caffeine, and Other Vices

There may be other, less direct benefits that an exercise program can bring to blood-pressure control, such as providing a substitute for less benign addictions. Exercise can be very valuable to anyone trying to quit smoking, for example, giving instant feedback on the physical improvements that come with quitting and a positive addiction to replace the old one. While quitting smoking may not reduce blood pressure, it can remove some of the danger of elevated levels.

For other people, exercise can also reduce the need for two other drugs, caffeine and alcohol, which are often blamed for high blood pressure.

Caffeine

Actually, caffeine may have been unjustifiably blamed where blood pressure is concerned. We know that in people who are not used to caffeine, the amount found in two cups of coffee can definitely raise blood pressure for two to three hours. We also know that since the body adjusts to caffeine, the effect disappears in regular caffeine users. So there is not compelling evidence that regular coffee or cola users need to stop if their blood pressure is high. However, some people may develop an increased sensitivity to caffeine, and it is certainly worth cutting it out for a time to see if your pressure comes down. Expect, however, a few temporary withdrawal symptoms, such as headache and a feeling of mental slowness. The body adjusts to the mental stimulation of caffeine, and regular users depend on it for normal mental function — which is one reason to quit, if you don't like being addicted.

Alcohol

The case against alcohol is somewhat more clear-cut. It has definitely been associated with elevated blood pressure, especially in people over age 45. The effect is fairly subtle, with two drinks per day increasing pressure by about 6/3 mmHg. Clinically, we have seen individuals with higher intakes than that show marked improvement in blood pressure when they went on the wagon. If your pressure is too high for comfort and you drink, on average, more than one cocktail, glass of wine, or bottle of beer a day, it would be wise to try reducing or stopping your drinking for three to four weeks and assess the effects, with your doctor, on your blood pressure. Take a walk to unwind!

Warnings

Exercise can plainly be useful to the hypertensive on a number of different levels: controlling weight, controlling stress, and perhaps having an independent effect in controlling the pressure. Is the next step, then, to give all hypertensives a blanket recommendation to exercise? Not quite. Obviously there should be some precautions. Most middle-aged Americans have some degree of blockage of their arteries. Under the circumstances, it's not a good idea to impose sudden demands for extra work on the circulatory system, particularly if there is an added risk from elevated blood pressure. You may be able to build up to a high level of activity over time; but it is very important for everyone over age 35 to start an exercise program slowly, and build up capacity gradually without straining the system.

Selection of Exercise

Certain types of exercise can actually raise blood pressure. In a healthy individual, this is not necessarily harmful, since pressure will quickly return to normal. However, if pressure is already high, or even borderline, the additional load could prove dangerous. Ten years ago, it probably would not have been necessary to warn people against hanging by their feet for long periods. Not too many people spent their leisure time upside down. Now, however, some do, making it advisable to warn them that this particular activity will raise blood pressure.

The same is true of weight-lifting and other muscle-building exercises. Although these exercises have a role in making people look better, or helping them perform better in a chosen sport, they do not themselves enhance health. And in people whose pressure is already high, they could raise it temporarily to hazardous levels.

What about aerobic exercise – the dancing, running, brisk walking, bicycling, and swimming that raise the heartbeat and temporarily increase the workload on the whole cardiovascular system?

Not so long ago, the average cautious physician would have advised all patients with elevated blood pressure (or indeed with any hint of cardiovascular difficulty) to avoid unnecessary activity of any type. Now the sight of ex-heart attack victims or even people with new hearts pounding along at full speed, the picture of health, has helped all but the most conservative physicians to modify their stand. Most will now "permit" at least a program of brisk walking. Many will encourage their patients to undertake a more vigorous exercise program, provided certain guidelines are followed:

- Anyone who is currently being treated for high blood pressure, or who has a history of high blood pressure, should check with a physician before undertaking any exercise more vigorous than walking.
- During exercise (including walking) those with a history of high blood pressure should monitor their heart rate periodically (see page 73).
- Always stop and rest if you feel out of breath, or if there is any dizziness or pain in the chest.
- Take the talk test: never let yourself get so out of breath that you can't hold a conversation without strain.

To Sum Up

- There aren't any reliable symptoms to tell you whether or not your pressure is too high. If you don't know it, have it checked before you start on any vigorous exercise program. Don't rely on drug-store machines (which are not always accurate), but have it done by a health professional, preferably more than once.

- Don't accept a verdict of "normal for your age" or "within the normal range." Ask for numbers, remembering that the ideal is 120/80 or less (the lower, the better). Anything over 140/90 should be taken seriously.

- If your blood pressure is elevated, and the doctor prescribes drugs, take them religiously. Even if you are also taking other measures to reduce the pressure (for example losing weight, cutting down on salt) don't stop taking the medication without being reevaluated by your physician

- If your blood pressure is elevated, be particularly cautious about starting an exercise program. It's wise to stick with walking until your pressure has come down, and your stamina has gone up enough to let you go faster without pushing your heart rate too high.

Given these precautions, a program of exercise could be the key to a long and cheerful life. It helps you remedy the problems – such as stress and overweight – that helped your pressure go up in the first place, and can provide a positive addiction that helps you face life without all that salt, tobacco, caffeine, alcohol, and empty calories – which, for your blood pressure's sake, you may decide to do without.

Contrary to most people's beliefs, the more overweight you are, the less food you eat because your body needs less energy to fuel inactivity.

Diet &

Darlene Dreon, *M.P.H., M.S., R.D., and* **Peter Wood**, *D.Sc., Ph.D. Ms. Dreon is nutrition director, Stanford Weight Control Project, SCRDP, and former nutrition editor of* Fit *magazine. Dr. Wood is professor of medicine (research), Stanford Medical School; associate director, SCRDP; and author of* The California Diet and Exercise Program. *Both are marathon runners.*

EXERCISE

The successes of twentieth-century technology have made us far more sedentary than nature intended. Our biological systems no longer have the stimulation they need to work as efficiently as possible and keep us fit. As a result, most of us experience expanding girth and attempt to counter this by reducing our calorie intake through dieting. Ironically, this is the most inefficient method of losing weight: When you diet, your basal metabolic rate goes down, and you burn fewer calories.

There's a general belief that slim people don't eat very much and that's how they came to be slim. In fact, the opposite is generally true: Slim people *often* eat a lot. And, contrary to most people's beliefs, the more overweight you are, the less food you eat because your body needs less energy to fuel inactivity.

Thus, the paradox: you can actually eat more and weigh less.

Diet vs. Exercise

Increased activity brings increased caloric need, and thus you can essentially eat more when you exercise. Those who diet by reducing caloric intake reduce the body's fuel supply, and while it is possible to lose weight this way, it's far less efficient than a regimen of exercise combined with a diet moderately reduced in calories.

It is interesting to look at this historically by comparing food consumption (or rather, food disappearance) figures around the turn of the century with today's figures. You'll find we were once a population that ate more but was less obese.

At the Stanford Center for Research in Disease Prevention, we sought to prove this thesis by dividing a group of overweight men into three groups: a control group; a second group which dieted and lost weight, but didn't exercise; and a third group which exercised but maintained the same level of food intake.

Both of the latter groups experienced a caloric deficit, one by reducing the number of calories taken in, the other by increasing the number of calories burned. The result? We were able to prove for the first time that overweight men who exercise can lose a substantial amount of weight – comparable to amounts lost by dieting – but without dieting at all.

Put simply, we discovered the no-diet diet.

What we've further discovered is that those who lose weight through exercise maintain their weight loss better than do those who lost weight by dieting. As a public health issue, it comes down to this: Do you spend time and money instructing overweight people to eat more cautiously or to exercise more actively? Our study indicates that behavioral changes relating to exercise are retained better than behavioral changes relating to eating.

Some people complain that exercise is a useless way to lose weight because you have to run from California to Boston to lose 20 pounds. There's some truth in that: If you exercise for a year, you may have indeed run the distance to Boston.

The Fats of Life

Did you ever wonder where those hidden fat calories are coming from? Let's look at a typical high-fat meal from a fast-food restaurant.

McDonald's

Food Item	Calories	Fat (gm)	Protein (gm)
Big Mac	563	33	24.5
Large French Fries	350	17	4.5
Chocolate Shake	383	9	10
	1,296	59	39

41% of the calories are from fat!

However, we don't recommend that you rely strictly on exercise and activity to lose weight, although many people rely strictly on dieting.

Another study we did was comprised simply of 70 people asked to exercise for a year. We measured their food intake, and it jumped soon after they got into the program and stayed at a higher level. Eventually we found that these sedentary, somewhat over-weight people were being converted to slim, exercising people who were eating more robustly. If nothing else, this is good news for farmers and the restaurant industry – they should be out ad-vocating exercise to increase their sales.

As increased exercise promotes increased calorie intake, you're more likely to consume an increased amount of nutrients. In an extreme example, Professor William Haskell of the Stanford Center for Research in Disease Prevention measured the caloric intake of the U.S. Olympic cross-country ski team and found that the men demand 5,000 calories a day and the women 3,500 — about twice the American average. While they're fueling that grueling activity, they're supplementing their bodies' vitamin and mineral needs.

Good News About Your Metabolic Rate

A simple equation: if you increase your metabolic rate, you burn more calories. It used to be thought that you would burn roughly 100 calories for every mile you ran. But it's not as simple as that anymore — and it's all good news.

Say a day's energy expendi-ture for a moderately inactive man is 2,000 calories, the total amount of what he's eating and burning in a day. If he goes out at lunch and runs six miles, his expenditure would go up to 2,600 calories (that becomes the food he can eat

Exercise Needed to Burn the McDonald's Meal of 1,296 Calories		
Swimming @600 cals/hour	=	*2.2 hours*
Jogging @462 cals/hour	=	*2.8 hours*
Dancing @384 cals/hour	=	*3.4 hours*
Golf @120 cals/hour	=	*10.8 hours*

containing the extra nutrients), and he's increased his metabolic rate during the time he ran.

But the metabolic rate doesn't immediately return to the level it was at before the exercise began. Barbara Frey-Hewitt, an exercise physiologist with the Stanford Center for Research in Disease Prevention, recently concluded a study that measured the residual effects of this type of activity. She found that energy expenditure continued up to 75 minutes after the activity ended. This means that our runner not only gained the benefits of the exercise, but also boosted his metabolism even after he finished his run.

In order to measure whether there was a significant difference in calorie expenditure achieved by different kinds of exercise, other participants in Hewitt's study walked during their lunch hour instead of running, Her results showed that just as the intensity of the activity increases, so do the benefits. Walking still provides a residual incremental effect, but it only lasted for 50 minutes afterwards, while with running, the metabolic rate after exercise was always higher than after walking. Given the ease with which a calorie intake/expenditure imbalance can occur, this added bonus of more strenuous activity becomes important.

Diet, Exercise, and Weight Loss

There's no magic formula for achieving your weight goal in conjunction with exercise. Everyone knows about the four basic food groups: dairy products, meats, vegetables and fruits, and grains — a good diet to follow as long as you don't overdo on dairy products and meats, which are high in fat content. Seek fiber and minerals. Avoid excessive amounts of the dietary villains: alcohol, caffeine, sugar, salt, and cholesterol.

The key is moderation and balance. A stalk of asparagus added to a meal of prime rib and ice cream does not adequately represent the vegetable group!

Balance is also important as a measure of what you take in compared to what you burn up. A small imbalance of more calories taken in than expended — even as seemingly inconsequential as a third of a banana a day — multiplies until the end of the year, when you've gained ten pounds.

If you plan to combine dieting with an exercise program to lose weight, it's important to follow some basic guidelines on what to look for and what to avoid.

First, is the diet safe? The recommended 400 calories per day of a recently famous diet was not safe. The problem with a great many diets is that they use the word "diet" in the caloric sense only, ignoring the broader meaning of the word: i.e., an overall beneficial mixture of foods that is good for you and will help you stave off chronic diseases and other health problems.

Second, is it effective and permanent? If you gain the weight back, do you start back on page one of the book? It's been well documented that yo-yo dieting produces metabolic changes that make it even more difficult to achieve permanent weight loss.

Other questions to ask: Does the plan lead to gradual weight loss, and does its overall focus promote fitness and exercise, not a permanent decrease in food consumption? And is it practical? Certainly barricading yourself in a "fat farm" for six weeks may teach you new eating habits, but is it financially feasible?

Finally, the most important question: Is the program enjoyable? If it's so horrible that you have to grit your teeth to stick to it, it's not going to work anyway.

In summary, then, we should not see permanent adherence to low-calorie diets as the healthy way to live in the modern

---

How to Determine Your Calorie Needs

1. Basal Calories =
Desirable Weight (pounds) x 10

2. Add Activity Calories
  a) Sedentary = Desirable weight x 3
  b) Moderate = Desirable weight x 5
  c) Strenuous = Desirable weight x 10

3. If you want to lose weight, subtract calories for weight loss
(a deficit of 500 calories/day will initiate one pound of weight loss/week.)

---

world. The active, fit, and healthy individual eats quite robustly, and is not constantly preoccupied with calorie counting. But he or she nicely balances that substantial calorie intake with regular, sensible exercise, and so maintains a good body weight, indefinitely, without the constant gains and losses of weight typical of inactive people who use dieting alone to control weight. But in addition to the amount of food we eat, the type of food is very relevant to our health and our ability to exercise regularly. This is the topic of the next section.

Eating and Athletic Performance

Eating for success in athletics is a topic that has, in the past, filled volumes. However, it doesn't need to. The issue of special food for special performance is not as complicated as some authors would have you think, because the differences between a good "athletic" diet and one that is suitable for the unathletic contingent of the population are not necessarily large.

It's true that there are certain tricks of timing that can be of value to the athlete – foods that should be avoided at certain times, or emphasized at others. But as a generalization it can be said that the best performance will come from a diet that is not extreme, and that follows quite closely the much praised "Dietary Guidelines" of the U.S. Senate's Select Committee.

Specifically, the increased energy needs associated with physical activity can be met by a diet containing 55 - 60% of calories from carbohydrates, 15% from protein, and 25 - 30% from fat. If that advice seems familiar, it is because much the same proportions are recommended for everyone. When looked at close up and in detail, though, there are some refinements that the athletic person would do well to consider.

Protein

Misunderstanding exists concerning the protein needs of athletes. There is no evidence that high protein diets (more than 2.0 to 2.5 gm/kg/day) will help to increase muscle strength. Physical training of the muscles will build greater strength, not additional dietary protein. Excess protein that is not used for energy is converted to fat.

Table 1. *Complementing plant proteins*

How to get Complete Protein

As a rule of thumb, combine one food from any two of these groups, and you will have a complete protein.

Grains	Legumes	Seeds
Whole-wheat bread, muffins	Beans	Sesame seeds
Spaghetti, noodles	Peas	Sunflower seeds
Rice	Lentils	Nuts
Corn	Peanuts	

Examples

Peanut butter on bread

Lentil curry on bread

Pea curry with rice

Bean soup with whole wheat bread

Chili beans with cornbread

Tostadas with beans

Zucchini stuffed with rice and beans

Baked beans with whole-wheat bread

Tahini on bread

Beans with rice

Also, any high protein vegetable served with milk will provide complete protein, such as cereal with milk, or rice pudding.

Beans

All types of beans—navy, pinto, ceci, and all the others—can present digestive problems, depending on the way they are cooked.

Here is a method of preparing beans which will rid them of their natural gassiness. First, soak the beans for at least three hours, and discard that soaking water. Then cover the beans with boiling water and boil at least 30 minutes. Throw out that water and rinse the beans well. Now you are ready to boil them again until tender, or add the other ingredients from your recipes.

If the diet lacks adequate sources of energy in the form of carbohydrate or fat, then protein from the tissues may be taken as fuel. The way to prevent this from happening is not to eat more protein, but to make sure that an adequate energy supply exists in the form of calories from carbohydrates.

If necessary, protein can be used as a source of energy – 1-2% of the total energy needed during normal exercise. But since it is very inefficient for the body to turn protein into fuel, increased protein in the diet will not increase endurance. Furthermore, a high-protein diet can lead to feelings of fatigue and nausea due to the waste products of protein metabolism.

The normal, adult protein requirement is based on 0.8 grams of protein per kilogram of ideal body weight, an amount easily met when 12 - 15% of total calories comes from protein. The only exception is if the individual is building muscles through an increase in training or weightlifting. Then the protein needs might be higher (1.0 to 1.5 g/kg bodyweight – or about the level of protein that the average American is already eating (70 - 100 grams per day). In other words, even though protein needs may be increased by physical activity, there is no need to take protein supplements – especially since an athletic person's diet is higher in total calories than the average, and thus contains more than its share of protein. Moreover, excessive protein may have deleterious effects, like dehydration and kidney complications.

Protein doesn't need to come from meat, with its high saturated fat and cholesterol content. Plant foods such as legumes, grains, nuts, and seeds can provide complete protein similar to that in meat, provided that two different types of plants are eaten so that the amino acid low in one can be supplied by another. (See Table 1.)

Fats

Fats represent a concentrated source of energy, providing over twice as much as protein or carbohydrate. Yet fat cannot be used exclusively as fuel, because the muscles cannot use fat as the main source of energy during short-term exercise. Additional fat in the diet will not replace glycogen stores or increase endurance. And even in the athlete for whom obesity is not a problem, excess dietary fat can pose a threat to health, increasing the risk of cardiovascular disease and some types of cancer.

Like everyone else, athletes should aim to eat little fat of animal origin and to avoid where possible commercial products made with "hydrogenated oil," or palm or coconut oil (often simply called "vegetable oil" on labels). These products are also highly saturated and can increase plasma cholesterol.

As a rule of thumb, all fats should be kept to a minimum. When they are needed, it is best to use the polyunsaturated oils (such as corn and safflower) and olive oil, which is now thought to have a cholesterol-lowering effect. Fish oil is now also thought to be beneficial, especially when eaten as part of the fish. Taken in capsules, however, it may cause diarrhea and have other side effects.

Carbohydrates

Extra calorie needs for the active person should come primarily from carbohydrate-rich foods in order to maintain the muscle glycogen levels necessary to fuel activity. Muscle glycogen (the storage form of carbohydrate) is especially critical during endurance activities lasting for 90 minutes or more.

Endurance can be enhanced by an appropriate glycogen-loading regimen; and fortunately for the athlete, these have become much more pleasant in recent years. Not long ago, the process involved starting a very-low-carbohydrate diet (50 - 75 grams daily) about a week before competition, coupled with hard training to deplete muscle glycogen stores. Then three days before the event, the athlete "loaded" glycogen into the muscles with a high-carbohydrate diet. The heavy workouts without carbohydrates often led to hypoglycemia and ketosis with associated nausea, dizziness, fatigue, and a risk of exercise-induced injury, while the sudden return to a high-carbohydrate diet often led to bloating and diarrhea.

It is now felt that the low-carbohydrate diet is not necessary and has obvious disadvantages. Endurance training by itself helps to stimulate increased glycogen storage, and a high-carbo-hydrate diet helps the process along. As a result, the latest glycogen-loading techniques are more civilized than they used to be.

One week before competition, while exercising as usual, the athlete starts to increase muscle glycogen concentration with a diet containing at least 55% of calories from carbohydrates. Three days before the event, the athlete then loads up, increasing carbohydrate intake to 70% of total calories. He or she will do little exercise during this phase, allowing glycogen storage to increase to two or three times normal.

Carbohydrate loading does not mean overeating. Total calories should remain the same, which will mean a reduction in fat and protein. For the best muscle glycogen synthesis, the car-bohydrates should be complex ones (from breads, pasta, cereals, grains, legumes, potatoes, and vegetables) rather than simple carbohydrates (such as honey, jam, soft drinks, cookies, candy).

In fact, these simple carbohydrates can hurt performance. If you eat them 45 minutes or less before you exercise, your per-formance will decrease because of increased insulin levels. High insulin levels will also inhibit the use of fat as a fuel source, which is an important factor in events lasting longer than 60 minutes. So eating candy bars prior to exercising should be avoided. Fruit also contains simple sugars. Although it contains enough vitamins, minerals, and fibers to make it respectable, it should not be eaten within 45 minutes of the start of exercise.

Vitamin and Mineral Supplements

Vitamin supplementation appears to be of little or no benefit to athletic performance in people who are well nourished – whether they are physically active or not. Eating more than the Recommended Dietary Allowance for vitamins and minerals does not enhance performance, and in some instances may pose health risks. Since physically active people typically eat more because of increased calorie needs, they automatically get more vitamins and minerals in their diets, which makes supplementa-tion even less necessary than for the sedentary population.

Testimonials claiming increased performance through supplements are not supported by scientific studies. The American Dietetic Association goes on record as saying it "does not recognize any unique ergogenic (ability to increase work capacity) values of products such as wheat germ, wheat germ oil, vitamin E, ascorbic acid, lecithin, honey, gelatin, phosphates, sunflower seeds, bee pollen, kelp, or brewer's yeast."

In fact:
- Megadoses of niacin increase the use of glycogen for energy and inhibit the use of fat, which could decrease performance in endurance events.
- There is no dietary requirement for pangamic acid (B-15) nor for carnitine (B-T), both claimed to improve the transport of oxygen to the cells and decrease fatigue. No evidence exists that there are vitamin functions for these compounds.

Iron

Sometimes iron-deficiency anemia associated with low iron in the diet is seen in female athletes or strict vegetarians. Endurance athletes may not absorb enough iron or have high iron losses through the intestine or urine. Special attention should be given to monitoring blood values which indicate low iron stores. Individuals who train hard and sweat heavily could also increase their need for iron, which is lost through the skin. In order to decrease the risk of iron-deficiency anemia, the athlete should:

- Eat enriched or fortified breads and cereals, and other iron-rich plant foods such as legumes and dried fruits.

- Eat a rich source of vitamin C with meals supplying iron to enhance iron absorption.

- Cook in cast-iron skillets occasionally. The iron in the pan increases the iron content of the food, especially if the food is acidic, such as tomatoes, vinegar, and citrus fruits.

- Remember that the iron in vegetable protein sources (non-heme iron) is poorly absorbed. Combine it with the heme iron found in animal protein, which aids non-heme iron absorption.

•Include lean meats in your diet.

Calcium

Females who engage in very strenuous exercise may stop menstruating, a condition known as athletic amenorrhea. Even though exercise normally increases bone density, amenorrheic athletes may suffer from calcium loss from bones because of reduced estrogen levels. A high-calcium diet similar to that prescribed for post-menopausal women, providing 1,000-1,500 milligrams per day, may be necessary to offset bone loss. For women who don't meet their calcium needs through food, calcium supplements may be advisable — provided the amount does not exceed the RDA (and provided you don't use bone meal or dolomite, which may contain toxic amounts of lead).

All females who exercise, regardless of menstrual status, should pay attention to getting sufficient calcium in their diets, since a national survey showed that 75% of women between the ages of 18 and 35 do not consume the RDA for calcium. High-protein diets are known to increase calcium losses. Young women who eat adequate calcium in their diets and exercise regularly can help prevent bone loss provided menstrual function is not compromised.

Salt

Sodium and chloride (salt) are the most abundant minerals lost in sweat. Salt tablets, once administered to athletes, are no longer recommended, since they draw water into the gastrointestinal tract and cause cramping, nausea, vomiting, and dehydration. Furthermore, there is no need for them: Our diets can easily replace the salt lost in sweat. Americans eat about 4,000 to 8,000 milligrams of sodium every day, considerably more than the recommended level of 1,000 milligrams per 1,000 calories (up to a maximum of 3,000 milligrams).

The commercial "thirst quenchers" advertised for athletes are not necessary to replace lost minerals. You would need to lose more than three liters of sweat (which might happen during a marathon) to make any electrolyte solution or salt tablet necessary; the small amounts of potassium lost during exercise can be replenished by a well-balanced diet, high in fruits and vegetables.

Fluids

In order to prevent dehydration, it is important to take adequate fluids before, during, and after exercise. The replacement of water lost through perspiration and respiration during exercise is critical to health and performance.

Water helps cool the body by absorbing heat produced during exercise. It also cools by means of sweat as it evaporates. When as little as 2% of our body's water is lost, performance decreases. Dehydration can cause fatigue, increased heart rate, heat cramps, and heat exhaustion or heat stroke. When you exercise, you lose about 1 liter of water for each 600 calories you burn. Since thirst is blunted following vigorous activity, athletes should weigh themselves before and after they exercise. Then they should replace lost sweat at the rate of 16 ounces of fluid for every pound they lost.

It is a good idea to drink plenty of fluid up to two hours before exercising (though not sugar drinks, which cause a decrease in blood glucose during exercise and hinder performance.) If you drink too much fluid *during* exercise, you can feel too full and uncomfortable. The rate at which fluids empty from the stomach during exercise depends on the volume, temperature, and composition of the fluid; normally, the stomach empties at a rate of about three cups per hour, so small amounts of fluid (four ounces) taken at 10-15 minute intervals during exercise will usually not cause bloating.

The ideal fluid replacement is plain cold water, since water is absorbed from the gastrointestinal tract faster than any other beverage. Sugar drinks may slow down gastric emptying time and produce a feeling of fullness. However, in events lasting longer than 90 minutes, carbohydrate supplements in the form of glucose polymer fluid may improve endurance. Though still in experimental stages, these drinks provide fuel for muscular work and empty from the stomach quite rapidly.

One or two cups of coffee (or the equivalent amount of caffeine in other forms) can affect performance. Coffee drunk before an event lasting longer than one hour can delay the onset

---

Diet and Exercise Tips

1. If you exercise regularly, you can lose a substantial amount of weight without severe dieting.

2. Vigorous exercise can boost your metabolic rate, even after the exercise has ended.

3. Athletes do not need to increase the protein in their diet.

4. Everyone should keep fat consumption to a minimum.

5. Simple carbohydrates (such as honey, jam, cookies, and candy–even fruit) can hurt athletic performance if eaten 45 minutes or less before exercise.

6. Physically active people do not need vitamin supplements, provided they are well-nourished.

7. Female athletes, vegetarians, and those who train hard and sweat heavily may be at risk for developing iron deficiency.

8. Females who exercise heavily and develop amenorrhea should pay attention to getting enough calcium in their diets.

9. There is no need for salt tablets or electrolyte replacement beverages (commercial "thirst quenchers").

10. In order to prevent dehydration, drink lots of plain, cold water before, during, and after exercise.

11. If you are participating in an athletic competition, do not eat for three to four hours before the event.

---

of fatigue by promoting increased use of fat for energy and delaying the breakdown of limited muscle glycogen stores. Caffeine, however, also has drawbacks. In some people, side effects include stomach upset, nervousness, headaches, and diarrhea. Caffeine also acts as a diuretic and increases water losses. (And since it is a drug, its use is not supported by the United States Olympic Committee.)

Alcohol should not be drunk on the day of a competition. Besides acting as a diuretic, alcohol impairs coordination and muscular reflexes. Alcohol in the blood during exercise inhibits the use of glucose for energy, which can make you feel tired earlier.

Pre-Competition Meals

We recommend that you not eat on the day of competition for three to four hours before the event. This will allow time for the stomach to empty and will help maintain blood glucose levels during exercise. The meal should be low in fat, moderate in protein, and high in carbohydrates such as grains and fruits. It should contain about 500 calories. High-fat meals slow gastric emptying time and therefore should be avoided. Don't eat sugar for the two hours before you exercise. If you do, it may cause a precipitous rise in blood glucose. Also avoid gas-forming foods and carbonated drinks which can cause stomach distress, but drink plenty of unfizzy fluids, up to two hours before exercising.

Family Meal Planning

There is no need to prepare separate meals and snacks for the family athletes in training. Active and inactive alike can benefit from the same types of food. The complex carbohydrates that provide the athlete's fuel are excellent for filling up growing children and teenagers without adding fat to their diets (see Table 2). Adolescents who are active will simply need more, and it's important to supply adequate food for the youth who is growing while also expending large amounts of energy in exercise. Physical activity coinciding with a growth spurt can make heavy demands for calories, protein, iron and calcium.

For a pregnant woman, it takes more calories to do the same activities because of the increase in body weight. Therefore, women who continue to exercise during pregnancy should eat enough calories to cover the energy cost of activity plus provide for the usual adequate weight gain during pregnancy. Extra fluids are important to cover the water lost during exercise.

The Diabetic

The value of exercise in diabetes is now widely accepted, but timing is important. In the diabetic, exercise enhances blood

TABLE 2.

Healthful Snacks For the Entire Family

BREADS AND CRACKERS
Whole-grain bread
Bagels
English muffins
French bread
Pita bread
Tortillas
Bread sticks
Rice cakes
Armenian cracker bread
Melba toast
Matzoh
Pretzels, unsalted
Rye crackers
Popcorn, air-popped
FRUIT
Fresh fruit
Canned fruit, packed in
  its own juice
Dried fruit
Unsweetened applesauce
SWEETS
Fig bar cookies
Ginger snaps
Graham crackers
Low-fat gingerbread
Low-fat quick sweet breads
Sherbet
Sorbet
Ice milk
Frozen tofu dessert
Fruit juice popsicle

DRINKS
Yogurt and fruit in blender
Skim milk with cocoa powder (not
  chocolate syrup)
Fruit juice
CEREALS
Shredded wheat, spoon size
  Puffed wheat, corn, rice
Low-sugar fortified cereals;
  whole grain and
  bran cereals
OTHER
Low-sodium canned soups
Low-sodium canned beans
Left-over baked potatoes
Plain or fruit-flavored low-
  fat yogurt
Unsalted nuts (use sparingly
  because high in unsaturated fat)
Part-skim mozzarella cheese
Low-fat cottage cheese
Ricotta cheese, part-skim
  Reduced-calorie, low-fat cheeses
Muffins
Water-packed canned tuna

glucose lowering. It is important to coordinate meal time, peak insulin reaction, and exercise to avoid hypoglycemia. The best time to exercise is after a meal, when there is plenty of blood glucose available. Plenty of carbohydrate solutions should be taken during exercise if activity occurs during the peak action time of insulin. Blood glucose monitoring and food adjustments may be necessary to adjust timing of exercise to individual needs.

Adjusting Your Family's Meals

It's one thing to plan improvements in nutrition: It may be harder to carry them out. Even though you know in theory what constitutes a low-fat, high-carbohydrate diet, it may be hard to achieve one day-to-day.

One technique is to start with a systematic assessment of what you and your family are currently eating — keeping a written diary if necessary. To get yourself started, try listing the foods you ate yesterday (see Figure 1). Check your food intake for the number and variety of fruits, vegetables, grains, milk, meat, and meat alternatives. Mark with a star those foods that are too high in empty calories, like sugar, fat, and alcohol. Circle foods you eat frequently that are high in salt. Even if you can't see much of a pattern after one day, your record will at least make you aware of some of the reasons why you ate what you did and under what circumstances. If you can keep up your diary for a week, patterns will emerge, and solutions to some of your eating problems should start to suggest themselves. You can then gradually start to make the changes that will result only in a healthier and more active family.

Food Diary (EXAMPLE)   Day 1   Date 1/12/88

Foods, Beverages & Additions	Description & Preparation	*Salt	Amount	Place
Breakfast:				HOME
GRANOLA	NATURE VALLEY	1	1/2 CP.	
MILK	2% FAT	1	1/3 CP.	
WHOLE WHEAT BREAD		1	1 SLICE	
MARGARINE	NUCOA, STICK	1	2 TS.	
GRAPE JELLY		1	1 TS.	
ORANGE JUICE	FROZEN, UNSWEETENED	1	8 OZ.	
COFFEE	DECAF.	1	6 OZ.	
MILK	WHOLE	1	2 TB.	
Snack: COFFEE	REGULAR	1	7 OZ.	OFFICE
IMITATION CREAMER	LIQUID	1	1 TS.	
DANISH PASTRY*	ROUND, 4" DIAM. X 1/2" HIGH	1		
GLAZE			1 TS.	BAKERY
RASPBERRY FILLING			1 TS.	
Lunch: SANDWICH:		1		NIVEN'S
RYE BREAD	OVAL, 5 1/2"L. X 4"H. X 1/4"TH.		2 SLICES	
LETTUCE			1 LEAF	
MAYONNAISE	UNKNOWN IF REAL		UNKNOWN	
LIVERWURST	2" DIAM. X 1/4" THICK		2 SLICES	
TOMATO SLICE	2 1/2" DIAM. X 1/4" THICK		1 SLICE	
BBQ POTATO CHIPS*	1 SMALL BAG	1	10 CHIPS	
MILK	WHOLE	1	8 OZ.	
Snack: APPLE	LARGE — 3 1/2" DIAM.	1	1	OFFICE
GIN & TONIC*		1	8 OZ.	FRIEND'S
PEANUTS	DRY ROASTED, SALTED	1	1/2 CP.	HOME
CRACKERS	TRISCUITS		6	
Dinner: CHICKEN CACCITORE:		3		FRIEND'S
CHICKEN	LT. & DARK MEAT, NO SKIN		3/4 CP.	HOME
	FRIED IN OLIVE OIL			
TOMATO SAUCE	ITALIAN		UNK. AMOUNT	
NOODLES	FLAT EGG		1 CP.	
PEAS	FROZEN, BOILED, COOKED W/BUTTER	3	1/2 CP.	
RED WINE*		1	8 OZ.	
POUND CAKE*	SARA LEE 2"X4" X 1/2" THICK	1	1 SLICE	
ICE CREAM - VANILLA*	DREYER'S	1	1/2 CP.	
CHOCOLATE SAUCE*		1	2 TB.	
Snack:				
COFFEE	BLACK	1	2 CP.	FRIEND'S
				HOME

*Amount of salt added at table? 1-none 2-light 3-medium 4-heavy 9-unknown

Your Food Diary

Day_____ Date_____

Foods, Beverages & Additions	Description & Preparation	* Salt	Amount	Place
Breakfast:				
Snack:				
Lunch:				
Snack:				
Dinner:				
Snack:				

Amount of salt added at table? 1-none 2-light 3-medium 4-heavy 9-unknown

*O*ne, *five, or fifty exercise partners
... no number is too small or too large... at
home or in the workplace.*

Exercise

WITH OTHERS

Exercise is just one of those curious things . . . It can be so hard to motivate yourself, but every time you do, you're glad you did. Fortunately, a lifetime of enthusiasm and motivation for exercise can be generated in a number of ways. For most people the answer is simple . . . other people! Think of how many people you know who share your desire to be fit and healthy. All around you, at home, at work, at school, in your clubs and organizations, there are people just waiting for the opportunity to exercise. Exercising with these people is a wonderful way to get excited and stay excited about exercise.

By its very nature exercise is social. You can only benefit by taking advantage of that. Besides keeping your spirits and enthusiasm high, exercising with others has added wonderful side effects. New friendships are made, and old ones strengthened, all the while time rushes by and exercise becomes easier and more enjoyable than ever before.

One, five, or fifty exercise partners – no number is too small or too large. Nor is there a right and wrong way to enjoy the social side of exercise. Some people exercise only occasion-

Fran Carl, M.P.H., *June A. Flora*, Ph.D., and *Edward Maibach*, M.P.H.
Ms. Carl is program manager for the Health Improvement Program at Stanford University and consultant to numerous corporations establishing work-site fitness programs. Mr. Maibach is a doctoral candidate at the Institute for Communication Research at Stanford. Dr. Flora is associate director, SCRDP, and assistant professor of communication at Stanford University.

ally with partners, while others always do so. Some have regular partners, while others have many and rotate among them.

Many people who find their motivation for exercise through their involvement with other people become what we call "exercise advocates." By structuring their exercise to include others, they manage to stay fit while at the same time helping others become or stay fit. In their own simple way, exercise advocates seem to be the Pied Pipers of the exercise world. They show the fit and the not-so-fit alike just how easy and fun exercise can be.

You may even be an exercise advocate without realizing it. Some exercise advocates are themselves quite athletic, others are decidedly not. They are young and old, women and men. Some prefer to help just one person at a time, while others lead the way for small or large groups. Some are natural to their role, while others seem to grow into it slowly. Their real commonality is that they find great enjoyment in exercise.

The following is a self-assessment quiz that will help you learn how much of an exercise advocate you are or can be. Even if you are the type of person who prefers solitude while you exercise, you may find this self-assessment of interest. It is meant to be more of a learning experience than a set of criteria to judge yourself by. Keep in mind that answering yes to almost any one of the items below means you are or can be an exercise advocate.

Section 1

Exercise Advocate Self-Assessment Quiz

For each of the following statements, circle the answer, YES or NO, that you think is an appropriate description of yourself.

I enjoy exercising regularly three times
per week or more.   YES   NO   (A)

I participate in group exercise
activities (e.g., aerobic dance).　　　　　YES　　NO　　(A)

I often exercise with others.　　　　　YES　　NO　　(B)

I invite others to join me for exercise.　　YES　　NO　　(B)

I have participated in community exercise
events such as races, fun runs, or walks.　YES　　NO　　(B)

I have been a volunteer at community exercise
events such as races, fun runs, or walks.　YES　　NO　　(B)

I belong to an exercise group such as a running,
walking, swimming, or bicycling club.　　YES　　NO　　(C)

I have organized more than three people to
exercise together at least once.　　　　　YES　　NO　　(C)

I have helped at least one person develop or
restart a regular program of exercise.　　YES　　NO　　(C)

I try to encourage close friends and family
members to get regular exercise.　　　　YES　　NO　　(D)

I try to encourage acquaintances and co-workers
to get regular exercise.　　　　　　　YES　　NO　　(D)

I have organized three or more people to exercise
on a regular basis.　　　　　　　　　YES　　NO　　(D)

I advise other people about exercise, such as
proper equipment, conditioning strategies,
or times and places to work out.　　　　YES　　NO　　(D)

I have organized an exercise event in my
community, workplace, or organization.   YES   NO   (E)

Section 2

General Health Activism Self-Assessment

Following is a list of activities other than exercise that are recommended for good health. (Keep these in mind when answering the next set of questions.)

- *Abstinence from tobacco use*
- *Proper nutrition (e.g., a low-fat, low-cholesterol diet)*
- *Weight management*
- *Stress management*
- *Moderation in alcohol use*
- *Safety measures (e.g., seat belt use)*
- *Medical screening (e.g., blood pressure measurement, cancer screening, and blood cholesterol assessment*

For each of the following statements, circle the answer, YES or NO, that you feel is an accurate description of yourself.

I make it a point to read
information about healthy lifestyles.   YES   NO   (A)

I follow the practices recommended
above for good health.   YES   NO   (B)

I have discussed at least two of the above
health topics with my family and/or friends
in the last month.   YES   NO   (B)

I have been a volunteer within the last year
for a community health event (e.g., a health
fair, the Heart Association, etc.).   YES   NO   (B)

I encourage my family and friends
to follow the practices recommended above
for good health.   YES   NO   (C)

I support my family and friends in
following the above recommended health
practices (by giving them information,
doing it with them, or rewarding them).   YES   NO   (C)

I have organized a health-oriented
event (e.g., a heart-healthy potluck).   YES   NO   (C)

I have organized an on-going health oriented
group (e.g., a weight-loss group,
or a quit-smoking group).   YES   NO   (D)

Section 3

---

*Now write a number between 1 and 7 that indicates how likely
you are to engage in the following activities in the next three (3)
months. A "1" means NOT AT ALL LIKELY, and a "7" means EX-
TREMELY LIKELY.*

Participate regularly (at least three times   _____
per week) in activities that contribute
to my fitness.

Maintain a healthy diet, productively   _____
manage my stress, and engage in other
preventive practices.

Discuss issues of a healthy lifestyle   _____
with family and friends.

Invite others to join me
in a workout.   _____

Participate in community exercise and
health events such as fun runs, walks,
or health fairs.   _____

Volunteer at community exercise and
health events.   _____

Belong to an exercise group such as a
running, walking, swimming, or bicycling club.   _____

Organize at least three people to exercise
together at least once.   _____

Organize at least three people to participate
in an exercise activity on a regular basis.   _____

Encourage friends/relatives to exercise.   _____

Advise other people about exercise,
such as proper equipment, conditioning
strategies, or times and places to work out.   _____

Organize an exercise event in my
community or workplace.   _____

Scoring Guide

On the first two sections of the quiz, give yourself 1 point for each "A" circled, 2 points for each "B," 3 points for each "C," 4 for each "D," and 5 for each "E." Add up the points for both sections and record them along with the total number of points.

Your Exercise Activism Score _____ out of 40 possible
Your Health Activism Score _____ out of 20 possible
Total Activism Score _____ out of 60 possible

Before discussing how to interpret these scores, it's important to point out that the relevance of your score is limited by your own feelings about being an exercise and health advocate. Now that you have a better idea of what exercise and health advocates do, you can judge for yourself if any of it sounds appealing to you. We recommend that you at least consider the benefits to yourself and others by being involved in some of the activities listed in the quiz. Most people find that these activities not only help them to stay fit, but also add a new and rewarding dimension to their exercise. This scoring system is designed to give you a rough indication of how active you currently are compared to how active you can be. Your score is not a comparison of you to other people but of the current you to the potential you. Remember, these scores are a rough indication only. You are the most qualified judge of your true level of exercise and health activism.

Total Activism Scores:	*Fitness Only:*	*Health only:*
Low 0-19	Low 0-13	Low 0-6
Medium 20-39	Medium 14-27	Medium 7-13
High 40-60	High 28-40	High 14-20

If your total score is lower than you would like, there are a lot of simple things you can do to increase it. Go back and review the activities listed in Section 3 of the quiz, keeping in mind two things. The activities are listed in ascending order of involvement. That is, as you go through the list, each activity is a successively more important contribution. However, all levels and types of involvement are useful and necessary in promotion of better health, as well as in raising your activism score.

Which of the activities listed in section 3, that you are not currently engaged in, have you rated as likely within the next three months (scores of 5 or higher)? These are the activities with which you can begin to improve your activism level.

Next, consider those items in Section 3 that you rated not as likely to engage in within the next three months (scores of 4 or less). There are three types of reasons that can cause low "likelihood" ratings: 1) low desire to engage in the activity; 2) "external" barriers to completing the activity; and 3) "internal" barriers to completing the activity. "Likelihood" scores caused by the first reason are unlikely to change, but low scores caused by the other two can. This will become clear as we explain the "external" and "internal" barriers that diminish your likelihood of performing the activities.

"External" barriers are factors external to yourself, such as lack of time or lack of access to people or other resources, that prevent you from engaging in an activity. "Internal" barriers are those within yourself, such as lack of necessary information or lack of confidence in your ability to successfully carry out the activity.

Now take a few moments to reflect on the "external" barriers that have contributed to your low likelihood scores. Make some notes to yourself on what those factors might be.

_____

_____

_____

Now think about and record how you can remove some of these "external" factors that prevent you from being a more active exercise and health advocate.

_____

_____

_____

Repeat the first part of the exercise with "internal" factors: What "internal" factors are stopping you from becoming a more active exercise and health advocate?

_____

_____

_____

We recommend two methods to help you overcome "internal" barriers. First, learn more about health and fitness and how other people approach their health and exercise activism. This book as well as the materials developed at the Stanford Center for Research in Disease Prevention can be most helpful (send for free catalogue–see card at end of this book). Second, we recommend taking small, achievable steps to becoming a more active advocate, and then building on your success. With each step you take you will learn and build your confidence.

Start by identifying the first step you will take in becoming more active, and then commit yourself to follow through on that activity in the next week or so. As a first step, you can complete the following contract:

"I will _____   _____
             (activity)   (date)

If you scored high on either the fitness or health scale and low on the other, keep in mind that the same type of activities that got you the high score on one scale can be used to improve your advocacy in the other area.

Exercising at Work

One of the best places to become an exercise advocate is at work. Work often consumes so much of our time that it's difficult to break away, but some people are successfully combining work commitments and exercise. They may arrive early at their place of employment to participate in stretching classes; or take a brisk walk or noontime jog on their lunch break; or stay for company-sponsored aerobic sessions after work.

For you, exercising at work provides a built-in cadre of companions for the rigors of exercise, as well as providing a relaxed arena for communicating work-related problems. For your company, exercise programs may improve morale and productivity and decrease absenteeism.

There are other advantages for the company as well: While it might be part of the corporate philosophy to promote healthful activity and attract new employees, exercise may also reduce future retirement costs of older workers and health care costs for everyone. Whether it goes by the title Corporate Fitness, Worksite Wellness, or Health Promotion in the Workplace, the benefits of workplace exercise are many.

Your company's commitment may be as limited as providing free aerobics lessons at the local YMCA, providing healthier dietary alternatives in the company cafeteria, or sending you to stress-management seminars on company time — or as expansive as building a company gym or organizing an incentive program to encourage exercise.

Nevertheless, you can create your own exercise program, no matter what size company you work for and no matter what type, size, or location of your place of work; options are available to meet any need. More than 50,000 U.S. companies already offer employee fitness programs, and some 500 have built corporate health facilities.

Determining Wants and Needs

Remember that while your program is geared for your fellow employees, it must keep the needs of company management in mind, too, since they'll be financing it. A company interested only in improving employee morale would sponsor a program different from a company aggressively determined to contain health-care costs.

Depending on the size of the company, you need to enlist the support of people like the personnel director, the medical director, or the occupational health and safety officer. Keep in mind that your program will eventually become part of the corporate structure, and that it might fall under one of these staffers' purview. Be sure to consult top management as well, such as the vice president for administration or the company president. You'll have to realistically discuss the goals of a fitness program with these individuals so that a discrepancy doesn't separate your expectations from theirs.

Many people will agree that a workplace fitness program would be fun and would encourage communication among all company employees. But you should guard against fostering false hope that the program is going to magically lead to improved employee health or a containment of health services use. Improved morale, improved fitness, and increased knowledge about health are realistic goals for any exercise program.

If you are serious about demonstrating changes in employee health status or cost containment, you'll need a rigorous evaluation method and a sophisticated tracking system to measure the results; this will involve the services of an experienced health program planner and an evaluation expert. Less ambitious goals require less expertise.

Once you've enlisted the support of someone to fund and perhaps oversee the program, you need to determine your co-workers interests. Circulate a survey to gauge whether or not they currently exercise; if they'd be interested in a company-sponsored program; what their preferred time of day and type of exercise would be; and if they're interested in other health promotion activities (such as nutrition, back care, stress or weight management, or programs to help them stop smoking). Tabulate these responses carefully. Even though you have administrative support, a company-wide program will never succeed without broad-based, company-wide employee support.

Be sure to survey the staff regarding the depth of their own exercise-related experience – chances are you may find former or part-time exercise instructors or even 10K race participants who would be willing to lead classes and organize events.

Planning the Program

The next step in the process involves tallying a list of the needs the survey has identified. If the survey reveals widespread interest in an aerobic dance class, is there a large room with a hardwood floor (but without a cement slab foundation) to accommodate it? Is there a carpeted room large enough for flexibility stretching? If the staff is interested in an exercise room, is there funding to furnish it? If jogging is the exercise of choice, is there an outdoor area available, or a track nearby?

Depending on the depth of interest and the variety of participants, you can tailor your program to be as diverse as you wish and include special programs such as:

- fitness testing (blood pressure, pulse, and flexibility measurements) and training programs
- exercise instruction in aerobics
- walking and jogging groups led by trained leaders
- special classes for older, overweight, or pregnant employees
- an incentive program using points, contests, and prizes
- workshops on facets of exercise such as stress management and injury prevention.

In Stanford's Health Improvement Program (HIP), administered by the Center for Research in Disease Prevention, the exercise component is the most popular aspect of the program. Both aerobic dance and swimming programs are offered for beginning, intermediate, and advanced participants. For those who choose simply to walk, we've formed a Walking Club. Members receive an information packet that contains maps of campus indicating the mileage between points of interest.

Running the Program

Once you have decided what and under whose aegis your fitness program will be, you need to decide how it will be administered. You may want to designate a staff member of the human resources or employee relations department to manage it, but you should also consider that in many cities outside agencies such as the YMCA, the American Heart Association, or the community hospital are experienced in setting up and running fitness and health promotion programs for companies and businesses.

Alternatively, if you're planning an extensive program, consider that the responsibilities may include coordination and/or purchase and installation of facilities and equipment; scheduling of activities and distribution of publicity; employee motivation; and program evaluation. In this event, you may want to consider hiring a full-time program manager to ensure its success.

Judging such a candidate can be difficult. He or she should naturally be experienced in the kind of program you're proposing and should also have an accredited degree or training in exercise physiology, health education, public health, or behavioral science, as well as a demonstrated knowledge of exercise principles and precautions.

Assessing the Program

Once the program is under way, it's time to survey the participants again, this time on an even more extensive level. You'll want to tally the number of employees participating, their age, the percentage distribution of sex and job classifications, what they like most and least about the program, and if they've been injured in any way.

Be sure to gauge the physical and administrative details as well. Do activities take place on schedule? Are they adequately publicized? Do the facilities suffice in terms of space and equipment? Are the instructors patient and knowledgeable? Most importantly, is the program fulfilling employees' expectations? Only by accurately tabulating reactions to the program can you continue to serve the needs of the employees, which may change as they become more fit.

The key to a successful exercise program is its regular inclusion in the day's activities. Combining it in some way with the work routine — and taking advantage of peer support and guidance — makes it that much easier to adhere to and enjoy a fitness program.

Most importantly, I had to stop fearing failure and the "what-if-I-don't-make-its" and just get out there and compete for the love of it.

The Diary

1962

All I could see was a blur of blue water and fuzzy light. There was no sound. Wet, cold, and frightened, I felt a thud as I kicked my dad's body next to me and, feeling claustrophobic, I scrambled frantically toward the wall. Next thing I knew, my hands groped for the gutter. I pulled my head clear, gasped for air, and screamed. This wasn't exactly fun, but part of a routine that most two-year-old South Florida children went through. We were all taught to swim to survive potential falls into the multitude of lakes, canals, and backyard pools that exist there. Hardly an auspicious start, it was a few years before I voluntarily ventured toward the water again.

Kim Carlisle, B.A.
Ms. Carlisle was a member of the 1980 U.S. Olympic Swim Team; Gold Medalist, 1971 World University Games 200m individual medley; two-time national collegiate champion as member of the Stanford Swim Team; and 1987 National Masters Champion and age-group record holder in 50- and 100-yard.

1966

In front of me, at eye level, was a wash of blue dotted by white splashes from the flutter kicks of what seemed to be hundreds of bare legs. My arm was wrapped tightly around the clothed leg of my father. As I looked up, squinting in the bright sun, I could see him calling times to the swimmers as they breathlessly reached the wall, only to ready themselves for the next distance in the series. From the dry safety of the pool deck I

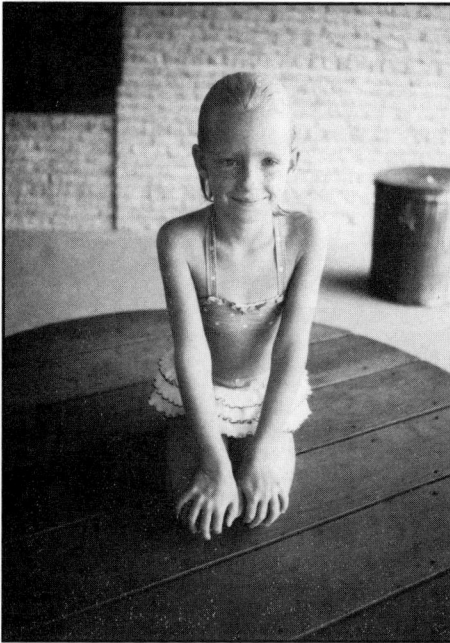

entertained the idea of what it would be like to be in the workout, to be part of the team.

It wasn't until 1968 that I added my legs regularly to that kicking frenzy and could watch my dad, Terry Carlisle, the head swimming coach at St. Andrew's School, yell to me from a distance.

This time it was love. I craved being in the pool. I had fun at practice. By now my parents had established a rule: We (my two younger sisters and I) could try any sport that we wanted to, but we had to stick with it for one year before we had the option to quit. They had set this up to allow us time to develop a skill and to learn to live with all the inevitable ups and downs. Without this rule, my youngest sister would have jumped all over the sports map and never given herself a chance to succeed at any depth. But I was hooked. Nothing could have coerced me to leave swimming — not even all the slumber parties in the world.

At age 8, I won my first race, the 50-yard breaststroke, and my practice schedule of five workouts per week, 1 1/2 hours each day, commenced.

1974

"Kim, I really think you can be great," I heard my dad say to me as we walked out of the pool on a breezy, humid night in Tallahassee, Florida. I was tired and hungry, and thinking about my teammate Randy, who had quit today. His father was always at practice and watched everything Randy did, even at meets. For that matter, so was mine, but somehow it was different. My father and I had an agreement; at practice, he was coach and I was swimmer. At home, he was Dad and I was daughter. We tried to leave each role in its proper setting and not bring one into the other. But Randy's father yelled if Randy swam poorly and bragged if he swam well. He never let up. It was no wonder to me, really, that Randy had quit. I could never have lived with that kind of pressure. It would have driven me right out of swimming before I even had a chance to test my ability.

Now Dad was telling me he thought that I had the potential to be a national, maybe even world-caliber athlete. Wow! This dream that so many kids had could become a reality for me. Goose bumps rose on my neck; my eyes got misty. At that moment, it struck me that Randy and I had embarked on two very different paths today, largely due to the support, and lack of support, of our respective parents. Though mine cared about what I did, they always reminded me that the choice to continue was my own. Intuitively, I knew that what my dad was telling me now was true. But it took his words to plant the seed of belief in me that I could do it.

School was almost out, and I was planning to start working out on a new machine called Nautilus — something few swimmers, especially girls, were doing yet. I would also be increasing my hours in the pool to 14 from 7 1/2 per week. Would this be the summer when I would first make Junior Nationals?

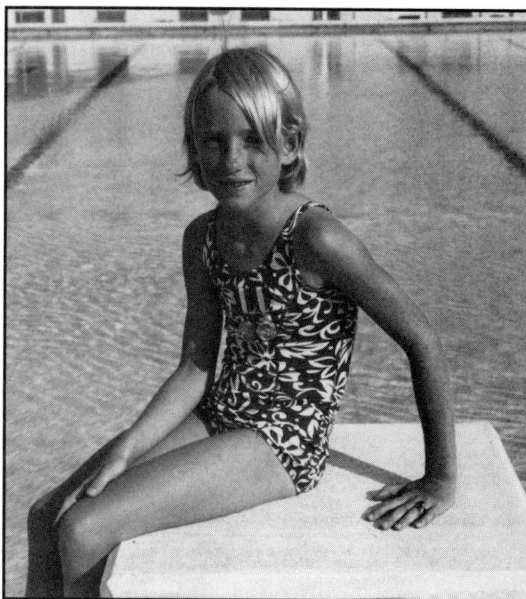

1976

Cap taut and close around my ears? Check. Goggles cleared and snug over my cap? Check. Straps on my navy lycra suit adjusted? Check.

The dark plastic of my swim goggles filtered out the bright afternoon sunlight. I swung my arms and jiggled my legs to keep the muscles loose. Outwardly, I knew that I appeared calm, but inside I was churning, hardly able to contain the volatile mixture of excitement and adrenalin. My throat was tight, and my heart pounded in my chest as I heard the announcer begin to introduce the swimmers in my heat. "Swimming in lane number five, 1976 Olympian Donnalee Wernerstrom. In lane number six, swimming in her first-ever U.S. championship final, 15-year-old Kim Carlisle." It was as if someone turned up the volume of my heartbeat several decibels. The announcer continued, "And in lane seven, another 1976 Olympian, in this event — the 200 IM [individual medley] Kathy Heddy." As he completed the introductions, I thought, "Wow, here I am — the fifth-fastest qualifier in my first national final and I am swimming next to not one, but *two* Olympians who had just come to Philadelphia from the Games in Montreal. Plus, this race was being broadcast LIVE by ABC *Wide World of Sports*; plus, minutes before, South African Jonty Skinner (who had not been allowed to compete in Montreal) set a WORLD record in the 100-meter freestyle." The air crackled and I shook in my bare feet as I climbed onto the block.

"This is the 200-meter individual medley — one lap each of butterfly, backstroke, breaststroke, and freestyle." Intermittent silence. "Take your mark . . ." The butterflies in my stomach subsided momentarily as I gained enough control to reach down to the front of the block and grab it on either side of my feet without falling into the water. Instantaneously, the cap in the starting gun ignited and set my muscles into reflex motion. The crowd erupted, water rushed past my ears, and then all was quiet. The race began.

For the next two minutes, twenty-two seconds, and some odd tenths, I felt like I was on automatic pilot — my mind was preoccupied with watching the splashes on either side of me; my body just seemed to know what to do. Somehow, the adrenalin carried me through the first three laps effortlessly. It wasn't until the final fifty meters that I settled in and discovered the pain in my arms, legs, and chest. But I was also close on the heels of my two Olympian neighbors, so I put my head down and stroked aggressively to the finish.

Fifth. Relief. The pressure was gone. It was as if someone had let the air out of my nervous balloon. It was my first appearance as a national finalist and I hadn't finished last! No, I had swum even a faster time than in the preliminary heats. I was so proud — I had won *my* race.

1978

I came off the seventh wall, arms streamlined overhead, legs still kicking strongly despite burning muscles and aching lungs. Every corpuscle in my body screamed for oxygen. Only twenty-two more strokes to the finish.

I could see people waving frantically along the side of the pool. But in the water it was silent, except for the "whoosh" of water as my hands stroked past my ears. I knew where my coach was, but I didn't want to look.

"Twenty-one, twenty-two . . ." My palm jammed the finish pad and I turned immediately to look at the giant scoreboard which flashed my time. Next to lane four were the numbers, "1:59.76." OH! WOW! Paradoxically, I could hardly believe my eyes, and yet I knew that, of course, it was right. "1:59.76" was the exact time, TO THE ONE-HUNDREDTH OF ONE SECOND, that I had mentally programmed and physically trained myself to perform in this very pool, this very race, this very moment. I was stunned, and exhilarated. It was the second-fastest performance ever by a woman in the 200-yard backstroke; I was the second woman in history to break the two-minute barrier. Finally, oh, finally, I had done it. I had arrived in the top echelon of U.S. and international swimming.

But, as it turned out, I was not yet ready for the high expectations that go with entry into this elite club, and my performance over the next year showed it.

After that race catapulted me into the aquatic limelight, high expectations and extreme pressure, generated by myself and others, weighed on me as I trained the following summer for the

World Championships. I was an obvious favorite to make the team and represent the U.S. in Berlin.

At the trials in August, I crumbled in the backstrokes, where the expectation was heaviest. Ironically, in the 100 and 200 freestyle events, I finished a surprising 6th and 7th, narrowly missing qualification for the 16-member women's squad. The final day of the meet was my last chance and best race — the 100-meter backstroke.

For days I had dreaded it; by the time I reached the blocks I was choked with fear. What if I didn't make it? What if my feet slipped on the wall at the start? I would be embarrassed, a failure. As the starter called us to the wall, I trembled. I couldn't wait for this to be over. "Take your mark . . ." Just as I had pulled up toward the block and tucked in toward the wall, the gun ignited. As I pushed off, my feet went straight down the wall. When I finally surfaced, well behind the field, I gasped for air. It was over then. For the next 97 meters, tears mixed with water as I struggled to finish, dead last.

There was a silver lining in this defeat, however, when I was asked, instead, to compete for the United States "B" team based on my performances in the freestyle events. We traveled to Montreal, Canada, to duel the Canadian "B" team in the 1976 Olympic pool. It was a relief not to have to compete in backstroke. I had a great time, explored Montreal, and met several new teammates who became long-term friends.

But that experience was not enough to assuage the disappointment of failing to qualify for the World Championship team. And, in spite of my failure, the expectations of myself, my

coach, and my peers were compounded. I really hated going to the pool now. For the first time in twelve years, I seriously contemplated quitting.

How could I even think about giving it all up — when in the fall of my senior year in high school, I was a top contender for a full scholarship to Stanford? My mind was a carousel of reason, then emotion, then fear and disappointment. Before I could stop it, I was in bed with mononucleosis, out of school for two weeks and out of swimming for at least three.

During that time, as I lay in bed watching my muscles atrophy, I made some decisions that changed my perspective on swimming, my relationship with my coach, Skip Kenney (who in the near future would become the men's coach at Stanford), and my life.

I wanted to swim, I didn't want to turn into a physical blob. Swimming had to become fun again; no more on-deck threats of "if you can't make this set, you'll never beat so-and-so." Instead, I needed to hear, "Come on, Kim , if you make this set, it'll be your best workout swim ever." Support and encouragement were more nourishing to me than loud intimidation. It was time to refocus my attention on the real values of swimming — being fit, challenging myself, learning to get along with my teammates, making new and lasting friends, and getting a chance to see a lot of the world by the age of 18. Most importantly, I had to stop fearing failure and the "what-if-I-don't-make-its" and just get out there and compete for the love of it.

Thankfully, Skip agreed and we made it work. After I regained my health, it took some months to put my new philosophy into practice. My self-confidence gradually returned as I developed the resiliency to make a comeback. I did. In 1980, the summer after my freshman year at Stanford, I made the U.S.

Olympic team in the 100-meter backstroke. Earlier that season, our collegiate team swam away with the national title, including my first individual championship ever in the 50-yard backstroke.

It wasn't until 1981, however, that I was able to repeat my sub-two-minute performance in the 200 back — exactly three years after the first time. From there, it was into the home stretch as I successfully completed my college eligibility with a second team championship for Stanford — one of the most treasured moments in my career.

In 1983, I decided to leave swimming as a full-time commitment and instead turn my attention to developing new areas of my life.

1987

Ten men stepped up, each to their respective starting blocks. Most sported graying hair, some were balding. They represented a variety of body types — tall and wiry, short and stocky. Several were beginning to show their years around their middles.

"Go, Dad!" I yelled to the swimmer in lane number five as they were called to their marks. This was heat #10 of the men's 100-yard individual medley, age 50-54, in the United States Masters National Short Course Championships. The setting was De Guerre Pool at Stanford University.

My eyes moistened and the adrenalin raced as I watched my father dive into the water to swim his first competitive laps since 1957. Boy, was this a change. For fifteen years, he had been watching me. So this is how he must have felt — anxious and excited and proud — every time one of his daughters raced. It was his turn to be the one cheered for — a moment certainly overdue.

In the final twenty-five yards, Dad pulled up on the field to finish second in his heat and tenth overall. As I ran over to congratulate him, I realized that my heat would be called in a few minutes.

My heat? I visualized myself on the blocks, preparing to race for 100 yards. Sensations that I hadn't felt for a long time suddenly stirred — anticipation, anxiety, excitement, doubt. How would I perform? Four years had elapsed since my last competitive swimming race. In the years following my retirement, I had worked to strike a balance between career, relationships, new athletic interests, and maintaining physical fitness. It took nearly eighteen months for my body (and mind) to adjust to reduced calorie output and food intake (some athletes seem to forget the latter and end up with significant weight gain), plus the new stresses of an office-bound job. Soon I found that if I didn't get some kind of exercise nearly every 36 hours, my mind would "fog" and I'd become grouchy. At the end of a work day, I often felt as if I needed to sleep. But if I exercised instead, the fog would lift.

So a weekly schedule of six days of exercise and one day off commenced. Rarely would I practice the same sport two days in a row. A mix of swimming, running, cycling, boardsailing, and tennis kept me entertained, fit, and energized.

In January of this year, I decided to commit myself to four workouts per week with the Stanford Masters team and get in shape for this meet, four and one-half months later. Soon, with business travel and volunteer projects, this schedule proved to be too draining. I dropped my attendance to two nights with the team, and one or two lunch-time swims on my own. During this stint, I never swam more than 4,000 yards in a single practice. Compared to ten workouts a week and up to 14,000 yards a day in my prime, that was very little training.

I had little reason to believe (based on what I was previously taught) that I had anywhere near the amount of yardage under my belt to support a quality performance in this meet.

But what was I here for? To win? No. I had firmly told

myself that my sole goal in swimming here was to participate and to have fun. Yet, as I waited behind the blocks, the competitive urges returned, and the desire to race, to win, prevailed.

"Swimmers, take your mark . . ." Once on the blocks, it was as if no time had passed since 1983. Now recalled, the mental skills seemed fresh. It was once again automatic and mentally effortless for me to perform.

My physical strength and conditioning held up surprisingly well, too, over the four-lap race. I finished second in 1:01.10, .01 seconds out of first place, and .02 from the national record. Based on this race, I figured that I had a shot at winning the 50- and 100-yard backstrokes on Saturday and Sunday.

Buoyed by cheering friends and family members (including my father, of course), and a combination of self-confidence, aggressiveness, and desire to win, I went beyond even finishing first. My times, 27.8 and 58.7, respectively, set national records in the 25 - 29 age group.

And I knew why I was successful. I had learned how to race and had not forgotten. Fear was absent; belief in my ability was present. Most importantly, I was having FUN.

Plus, Masters swimming is magnetic: The sheer number of people who participate (2,300 in this meet — the largest in U.S. history), the noise, the energy, and the aura draws you to it, and only reluctantly lets you go. Days later I heard stories from friends who had walked by the pool (not knowing what was taking place), stopped to watch for a few minutes, and stayed for hours. My mother and sister, who had hung around many long, tedious, swim meets in their day, were fascinated, even though this one was the longest of them all. Several "serious," world-caliber Stanford swimmers timed heat after heat in the hot sun. I couldn't imagine why they were willing to spend so much precious weekend time at yet another meet. George Haines (the Stanford coach and Masters meet organizer) must have coerced them. "No, Kim," one of them corrected me. "It is an inspiration for me to witness this. All of my peers should. It would renew their enthusiasm for swimming and reduce our fear of growing old."

In the Masters meet, gray and white heads were as common as brown and blonde. There were as many heats in the 50+ age groups as in the 30+ category. Children rode around the pool deck on their fathers' shoulders or in their moms' backpacks. Grown men and women cheered for their parents and grandparents. I was as excited to see an 80-year-old man step up to the blocks and swim a 50-yard breaststroke as I was to set a national record for myself.

Winning was part of the meet, not the focus of it. As I left the competition pool to swim down in the diving well after the 100 backstroke, a strange feeling overcame me. What was it? Disappointment? Couldn't be — I had just swum an excellent race. The normal post-race letdown? Maybe. Then it hit me. In every national championship I had ever participated in, placing first was most important, topped only by breaking an American record. After your race, you were always congratulated, usually interviewed by the press, and awarded by ceremony. The aura lingered. Here, winning was honored and appreciated, but only until the next heat was on the blocks. Then attention turned to the next swimmers— it was their moment to be in the limelight. I found this change rejuvenating.

It is time for U.S. coaches and young swimmers to pay attention to what is happening in Masters swimming. Participation is valued most, closely followed by fitness and the challenge of learning to race. It's not for the glory, the medals, or the ego, but for self-reward.

Most men and women I talked to had not trained much more than me. And they were swimming fast — national records were set in almost every age group in nearly every event. Countless numbers, from age 25 to 60, continue to swim faster today than they did in college. My time of 58.7 in the 100 backstroke was three seconds off my personal best of 55.7, set six years ago. But compare 58.7 seconds and four months of training, swimming no *more* than 10,000 yards per week, to 55.7 seconds and many years of intense training and weightlifting, swimming not *less* than 50,000 yards. That means that I swam 94% of my previous best on 20% of the yardage.

Are we grossly overtraining our young athletes today? (Many swim up to 10,000 yards per *workout*.) Wouldn't less swimming and more cross-training in compatible sports (cycling, running, cross-country skiing) prevent burn-out and maintain perspective and enthusiasm? Isn't having fun in your sport the primary reason to participate? Shouldn't a larger percentage of practice time be spent on visualization (mental rehearsal) and developing racing skills? Granted, like learning to drive a car, it takes a certain amount of physical practice to make a skill mentally automatic. When, in swimming, do we reach a point of diminishing return?

Based on my experience in the Masters Nationals, I would answer a resounding "yes" to the first four questions and urge that serious consideration and study be given to all.

Toward the end of the final session of the meet, I began to think about what I had done and where I wanted to go from here. Someone asked me if I would try to make the team in '88. "The Olympics, you mean?" I was surprised. "No. But, thank you. That chapter of my life is closed." Would I train for the next Masters Nationals? Should I chalk this up to a fun experience and take a break from swimming again?

My daydreams were interrupted when I bumped

into Laura Val, a 35-year-old nurse and mother of two who had set five national records in this meet. We had trained together at Stanford since January and I, the 27-year-old, was the one always trying to keep up with her. In fact, I didn't believe she was 35 until I saw her driver's license. "Laura, are you going to take a break for awhile?" I asked, still contemplating what to do. "No. I swim to stay fit, not just for the meets. I'll be at workout on Tuesday."

That was the difference! These men and women have made swimming a sport for life, rather than living for swimming, as I did for 15 years. If this woman could swim her best times ever at 35, practice a full-time career, spend time with her family, and still devote three or four evenings a week to the pool, then, by comparison, I had no excuse.

On Tuesday, I was at practice, too.

The short answer is that regular exercise does indeed reduce the risk of premature death considerably.

Long Life

Does exercise help people live longer? Or does it only seem to?

In the previous chapters of this book, my colleagues have argued that, far from detracting from the quality of life, physical activity will unquestionably enhance it. But to answer the first question — whether exercise actually prolongs life — I will present you with some data derived from a study involving nearly 17,000 Harvard alumni, over a period of many years.

These observations began in the early 1960s as part of a larger effort sponsored by the National Heart Institute and designed to assess the long-term health effects of lifestyle elements of college students and alumni.

At the core of this survey were questions

> *Ralph S. Paffenbarger Jr.*, M.D., *is professor of epidemiology, Stanford University School of Medicine, and visiting lecturer on epidemiology at Harvard University School of Public Health. He has completed 18 Boston marathons, and 5 Western States 100-mile runs.*

designed to measure the men's current levels of physical activity. They were asked to report how far they walked in an average day — with 12 city blocks equaling one mile. They reported on flights of stairs climbed, with 10 steps equaling one flight. They told us of any light, moderate, or heavy sports play that they regularly engaged in, including gardening and work around the house or garage.

On the basis of their reports, we then computed the total amount of energy that each man expended each week in terms of the number of kilocalories, or calories, used up at the following rate:

Stair-climbing		40 kcal per 100 steps, up and down
Walking		100 kcal per mile (12 blocks)
Sports	— light	5 kcal per minute
	— moderate	8 kcal per minute
	— heavy	10 kcal per minute

Since we wanted to measure the effectiveness of exercise in reducing risk of premature death in the presence of several other factors, we also inquired about their state of health, including questions on smoking and drinking patterns, family health history, and specific chronic diseases, including hypertension. In addition, we checked their student health and athletic records to find out their state of health as freshmen and whether or not they had participated in varsity or intramural sports during their four years in college.

Some 20,000 alumni furnished us with the information we had requested, and, excluding those who had evidence of coronary heart disease at the beginning of the study, we have been following their progress ever since.

Regular Exercise Reduced Risk of Premature Death

Our first major analysis of the relative effectiveness of exercise on longevity came in 1978, by which time 640 alumni had died of cardiovascular disease. We were able to correlate the relative risk of premature death with their contemporary exercise patterns and other personal characteristics in the men's lives.

And what did we find? The short answer is that regular exercise did indeed reduce the risk of premature death considerably. Men who expended 2,000 or more kcal a week in exercise had a rate of premature death from all causes that was 28% less than that of their sedentary counterparts in a 16-year period of observation. This translates into one to two years or more of extra life; not immortality, to be sure, but at least a postponement of that fateful day.

Most of the difference in mortality between active and sedentary alumni can be accounted for by the reduction in heart disease, which was apparent in all groups of exercisers, including those whose risk was elevated by other risk factors such as smoking, hypertension, and a family history of short survival.

For example, our data show, as you would expect, that cigarette smoking increased the risk of coronary heart disease considerably. If none of the alumni had smoked cigarettes, the death rate from heart disease would have been 25% lower in these 16 years (see graph).

When you add exercise to the equation, the risk was reduced significantly. A moderate smoker (up to a pack a day) who expended 2,000 kilocalories a week in exercise would still have more risk of heart disease than a nonsmoker; but his risk was about half that of a moderate smoker who had little or no exercise.

A similar observation can be made for hypertension. While high blood pressure in general increased risk by 118%, much of this extra risk could be offset by exercise. Those hypertensives who expended more than 2,000 kcal a week in exercise had less than half the death rate from cardiovascular disease of their sedentary contemporaries.

Parental history of heart disease provides an even more striking example. A sedentary alumnus with cardiovascular

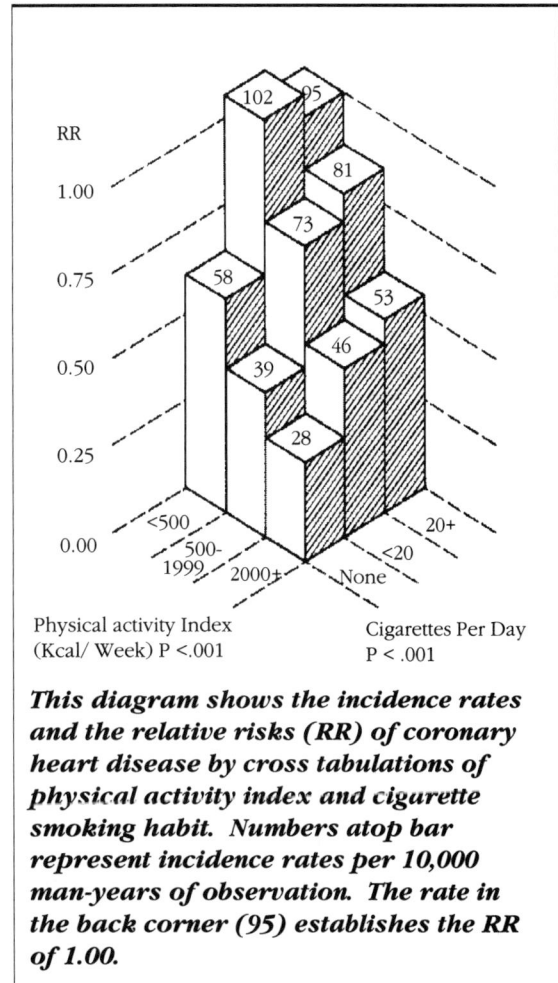

Physical activity Index
(Kcal/ Week) P <.001

Cigarettes Per Day
P < .001

This diagram shows the incidence rates and the relative risks (RR) of coronary heart disease by cross tabulations of physical activity index and cigarette smoking habit. Numbers atop bar represent incidence rates per 10,000 man-years of observation. The rate in the back corner (95) establishes the RR of 1.00.

disease on both sides of his family doubles his own risk of coronary heart disease. An active one, expending at least 2,000 kilocalories a week, would essentially neutralize his genetic risk completely. Indeed, his risk would be lower than that of a sedentary alumnus with no heart disease in his family.

How much exercise?

The figure of 2,000 kilocalories a week that we used as a basis for many of our observations is in a sense an arbitrary one, but it represents a level that produces significant benefits without demanding a full-time devotion to exercise. Without knowing how much exercise occurs as part of your normal routine, it is hard to predict with any precision how much daily exercise you would need to expend energy at the rate of 2,000 kcal a week. However, if you spent the rest of the day in bed, you would achieve that goal through any of the following activities, in any combination that you wanted:

> 57 minutes a day of light sports play
> 35 minutes a day of moderate sports play
> 28 minutes a day of vigorous sports play
> 2 3/4 miles of walking a day
> Climbing up and down 800 steps a day (some 40 stories of a modern office building)

Unless you have to climb a remarkable number of stairs each day, or commute considerable distances on foot, you will probably need to include some regular participation in sports if you are to achieve a useful expenditure of kilocalories. And indeed, two thirds of the alumni who expended 2,000 kcal or more did it with the help of some type of regular sports activity.

Sports featured even more prominently in a study conducted by a distinguished British researcher, Dr. J. N. Morris, who asked 18,000 civil servants to record what they did every five minutes on a given Friday and Saturday – in other words, on a work day and one spent (presumably) at leisure. He then correlated their reports of energy expenditure with their risk of developing coronary heart disease.

Dr. Morris found that for his civil servants it took vigorous exercise to reduce the risk of coronary heart disease — in particular the type of repeated and sustained exercise common in sports play. Other vigorous activity the civil servants reported, such as dismantling a car engine, or cutting down trees, did not correlate with reduced risk: after all, there are only so many trees that can be cut on an average piece of property, so such activity would not be sustained on a regular basis.

Even if you already maintain a high level of exercise by climbing stairs or walking blocks, there is certainly no reason to exclude sports. In general, the studies found that the more activity you can include in your life, the better. Although we have used the figure of 2,000 kcal extensively in our calculations, there is no particular magic to this figure. Any activity (even as little as 500 kcal a week) is better than none, and the benefits will increase steadily up to a level of 3,500 kcal a week, and possibly much further.

Selection vs. Protection

At this point, you may be pondering two questions which occur to many as they weigh the supposed benefits of exercise: Are people healthy because they exercise, or do they exercise because they are healthy? These are questions which obviously have a bearing on the value of exercise in prolonging life expectancy. They can be broken into four more specific questions:

1. Are sedentary people sedentary because they are ill?
2. Are active people active because they are healthy?
3. In contrast, are ill people ill because they are sedentary?
4. Are healthy people healthy and happy because they are active and fit?

For some people the answer will be mixed. They will not all fall neatly into one category or the other. However, after considering all the evidence, I think that we must conclude that exercise does offer protection against specific illnesses. Generally speaking, people do not exercise because they are healthy; they are healthy because they exercise.

There are many facts to support this contention:

• The association between exercise and reduced risk of coronary heart disease is strong and consistent. It is consistent by age, by race (white and black in studies of San Francisco longshoremen) and by sex (long-term studies of the population of Framingham, Mass., and studies in Finland and Holland have shown that both males and females benefit from the protective effects of exercise).
• Exercise makes an independent contribution to the delay of coronary heart disease and to the prolongation of life whether or not an individual smokes, has high blood pressure, is obese, or has weight that goes up and down. The benefit of exercise is independent from adverse family history, from high or low cholesterol, and from abnormal glucose metabolism.
• The relationship between exercise and risk of coronary heart disease is persistent in successive increments of time. In other words, what is true for, say, three years will remain true for the next three years, and the next.
• Finally, it makes common sense to believe that exercise can increase life expectancy and delay disease. It is consistent with the physiology of exercise and with experimental studies on laboratory animals. For example, the work of Dieter Kramsch of Boston College has shown that monkeys who were exercised for two to three years had less atherosclerosis, better lipid profiles, and fewer electrocardiographic abnormalities than monkeys who were not exercised.

Those studies that have been adequately designed and properly executed show the same thing: Active people are at lower risk of heart attack. In general, studies that have produced contradictory findings were in some way deficient. Perhaps they over-looked the fact that to be effective, exercise must be regular and constant. Physical activity patterns of years ago will not help you now; nor will exercise that lasts only for one season of the year, or for one day of the week.

We all know people who will seize on any excuse to avoid exercise. One of my favorite excuses is the "limited heart-beat" theory, whose proponents maintain that we are allocated only so many heartbeats in life. Since exercise raises the heart rate, they say, it will plainly shorten life and use up our precious allocation of heartbeats sooner than is necessary. However, these arguments can easily be refuted. As I have computed many times, the net effect of exercise is a reduction in the number of heartbeats per year. Even though the pulse may quicken during exercise itself, the resting heartbeat of a fit person becomes slower and more sedate, so that even if the heart rate is elevated for three hours a week, the net savings would allow for several extra years of life.

When the report on the Harvard alumni study was published in the *New England Journal of Medicine* in 1986, a distinguished colleague from the University of California made a lightning calculation and concluded, "The bad news is that although you may live an extra couple of years, those two years will be spent jogging." Put like that, the prospect may sound grim; but of course it is misleading. Our calculations show that a 40-year-old man who exercises for three hours a week, with a total expenditure of 2,000 kcal each week, will earn more extra life than the time he spends exercising; for each hour of exercise, he can expect 1.95 hours more life than his sedentary counterpart. Furthermore, his quality of life, as well as its length, will be enhanced.

Index

carbohydrate loading, 44, 143-44
carbohydrates
>complex, 46
>metabolism of, 12-13
>needs of athlete, 143-44
>percent of diet, 44, 140
cardiovascular endurance, 22-26, 57-61, 69, 70-71
cardiovascular training effects, 57-58
cellulite, 41
cholesterol, 13, 38
clothing, 104
commitment, 92
cool-down, 71-72, 103-4

dehydration, 42, 46, 147
depression, 14, 114, 121
diabetes, 12-13, 97, 149
diet, 135-53
>athletic performance, 140-49
>exercise, 135-37, 138-40
>food diary, 151-52
>meal planning, 149-50
>snacks, 153
>weight loss, 135-40

endorphins, 14, 128-29
endurance
>blood pressure, 13
>carbohydrates, 44, 143
>cardiovascular, 22-26, 57-61, 69, 70-71
>exercises, 19-22
>tests, 61-62
>equipment, 104-5. *See also* weight training machines
estrogen, 146
excuses for not exercising, 83-95
exercise advocates, 156-63

fats, 140, 142-43
fat weight, 28-30
fitness, 17-18
fitness log, 65
flexibility, 26-28, 62-63, 70
fluids, 45, 147-48. *See also* thirst quenchers; water

iron, 43, 145
isokinetic exercise, 21-22
isometric exercise, 19-20
isotonic exercise, 20-21

jogging, 76

life span, 37, 183-89
logs
        daily exercise training, 81
        daily stress and tension, 119
        food diary, 151-52
        monthly fitness, 65
        weekly activity, 64
low-density-lipoprotein cholesterol (LDL)

maximal oxygen consumption (VO_2max), 22, 24, 58-61, 73
maximum heart rate (MHR), 24, 26

medical evaluation, 49-50, 68-69
menopause, 11-12
metabolic rate, 9-10, 128, 137-38
minerals, 45, 144-46. *See also* calcium
motivation, 155
muscle mass, 10-11
myths about exercise, 33-47

obesity, 54-55
osteoporosis, 11-12, 99-100. *See also* bone density; calcium
overuse syndrome, 98-101

pain, 35, 36, 105-6
performance and diet, 140-49
physical limitations, 92-93. *See also* specific conditions
plantar fasciitis, 107
potassium, 146
precautions, 114-15, 130, 131-32
pregnancy, 149
programs, exercise
       group, 155-67
       personal, 67-81
protein, 44, 140-42
psychological benefits of exercise, 14-15

push-ups, 62, 69

range of motion. *See* flexibility

salt, 45, 126, 127, 146
scheduling exercise, 36, 85-87, 122
shin splints, 107
shoes, 104-5
sit-ups, 61-62, 69
smoking, 40, 185
snacks, 153
spot reducing, 40-41
sprains, 107-8
strains, 106-7
strength
        defined, 18-19
        exercises for, 19-22, 69-70
        protein, 140
        tests, 61-62
stress, 117-23
        causes, 117-18
        daily stress and tension log, 119
        endorphins, 14, 128-29
        exercise, 14, 121-22
        high blood pressure, 126, 128-29
        management strategies, 118-20
        signs of, 118
stress fractures, 99
stretching
        ballistic, 27-28
        cool-down, 71, 72, 103
        static, 27
        warm-up, 71-72, 101-3
stroke, 51-53
sugar, 46
sugar drinks, 147
sweating
        body cooling, 147
        salt loss, 45, 146
        weight loss, 42
sweatsuits, 42
swimming, 12, 77

Acknowledgements

Editor: Susan Wels
Contributing Editors: Prudence Breitrose, Howard Baldwin
Art Director and Illustrator: Tom Lewis
Production Coordinator: Bill Merz

Editor-in-Chief: Della van Heyst
Editorial Consultant: John O. Green

Acknowledgements:
Typesetting and Production were executed on Apple Macintosh SE, Microsoft Word 3.01, Aldus PageMaker 2.0a, and Adobe typographic fonts, with assistance from Hubert Cheng. Printed by Malloy Lithographing, Inc., of Ann Arbor, Michigan.

196

Credits

We thank the following for the use of the illustrations that enrich this book:

Cover ©Craig Aurness/West Light
page 8 ©Alma Boutiques
page 16 ©Insight Magazine/Sharon Roy Finch
page 32 ©Steve Murray
page 46 ©Garry Brod Photography
page 124 ©Barry Winiker
page 154 ©John Blaustein, ©Stephen Simpson

For your ongoing fitness efforts, the ideal companion to this book is . . .

The STANFORD Health & Exercise PROGRAM

(120-minute videotape)
Item MSTA0084 • 1/2" VHS • $39.95

In this videotape renowned fitness specialists team up with world-class athletes to introduce the concepts and practical tools found in *The Stanford Health & Exercise Handbook.*

The videotape:

- summarizes the eight prime benefits of exercise determined by the research of specialists at the Stanford Center for Research in Disease Prevention;
- presents four self-assessment tests you can use to determine your muscular strength, flexibility, and cardiovascular fitness; and
- features the Stanford Workout, for people who want to get in shape, stay in shape, or supplement their current sports and exercise programs. This unique video demonstrates three low-impact aerobic workouts—for beginning, intermediate, and advanced levels—simultaneously! You can use the fitness self-assessments to determine which level is appropriate for you.

Another unique feature of the video is a series of vignettes from five world-class athletes and former Olympians: Eric Heiden, Nancy Ditz, Roscoe Tanner, Kim Carlisle, and John Brodie. They show you how to prepare for sport participation so you can play safe, improve your performance, and enjoy sports for years to come!

Use the handy postage-paid Reply Card in the back of this book to place your order today!